EXCEPTION/ALL
An anthology exploring what it means to be normal

Exception/All: An Anthology Exploring What It Means to Be Normal

Copyright ©2023 by Northern Colorado Writers dba Writing Heights Writers Association

Cover Design: Leia Sage Creations
Interior Design: What If? Publishing

Print ISBN: 979-8-218-24284-8
Ebook ISBN: 979-8-218-24285-5

EXCEPTION/ALL

An anthology exploring what it means to be normal

Writing Heights

WRITERS ASSOCIATION

Table of Contents

Introduction 1
A Recipe for Normal* • Sandra McGarry 5
The Orange Tree • Katie Lewis 6
Sitting in poetry class... • Megan E. Freeman 17
Elegy for a Hawthorne • Janet Kamnikar 18
aka Estate Sale • Celia Turner................................ 20
Cleave • Celia Turner 21
The Incredible, Uncanny Interview! • David E. Sharp 22
Fakers • Emily Rodgers-Ramos.................................. 30
Art Modeling / Post-Fire Succession • Charlotte Suttee 31
Channeling the Vice President • Warren Jonsten............... 32
What Matters Most • Mary Kay Knief............................ 34
The Conformist • Carol A. Fichtelman 36
Even the Latest Telescope Can't Tell Us • Linda Whittenberg....... 44
Adam's Apple • Sam Shada 46
Pandemic Lover • Charlotte Suttee 48
A Sonnet for the Pandemic of 2020 • Belle Schmidt............. 49
The Touch • Mary Kay Knief 50
Hand-Written Letters • Sandra McGarry......................... 52
Median • Michael Pickard...................................... 53
Conversations with Sor Juana Ines de la Cruz • Gia Nold....... 61
Aftermath • Valerie A. Szarek................................. 62
The Wall • Leni Checkas 64
Refusing Meds, He Calls Obsessively • Lew Forester 66
Not Clinically Significant • Tara Szkutnik................... 68

Canaries • Mike Kanner..70

Tone of Voice • Lynette Moyer.....................................84

Misplaced Persons • Lynette Moyer.............................85

First, I must forget myself... • Charlotte Suttee..................86

Love with Oven Mitts • Lew Forester...........................87

The Grindstone • Lynette Moyer...................................88

Summer of Love: A Memoir • Jacqueline St. Joan................90

Morning in the Penultimate • Janet Kamnikar.....................100

Things to Do While Trying to Fall Asleep • Lynda La Rocca........101

In the Secret Room • Mary Kay Knief.............................102

When the Crabapple Blooms • Linda Whittenberg................103

In a Previous Life • Janet Kamnikar..............................104

My Lancelot • Megan E. Freeman..............................105

Notorious • Sunny Bridge...106

The Ice Cream Truck: Normal in an Un-Normal World............107
Anne Therese Macdonald

Homecoming • Mary Kay Knief...................................116

and another thing they never tell you... • Megan E. Freeman.......117

Going Under • Lynda La Rocca...................................118

Backing Out of the Driveway • Sandra McGarry.................120

The Slow Cloud Days • David E. Sharp...........................121

Tadasana • Celia Turner.......................................124

It's Easy to Be Normal • M. D. Friedman.........................126

Bios..129

    Editors..130

    Poetry Team...131

    Contributors..131

Acknowledgements..137

Introduction

The pandemic knocked everyone back. Whether you caught the early long-haul version (I did, so physically normal is a distant horizon) or you were hit with the Omicron, it still feels like we're hanging out in limbo. There's rhetoric about the new normal. There's clamoring to go back to normal. I posit that no one can actually define normality. I don't know many people who feel representative of normal. Of course, I'm a writer. None of us are normal by any standard.

And yet, we laud the exceptional. Denotatively, *exceptional* is troubling in its own space. Unusual, not typical. Unusually good, outstanding, or special. Deviating from the norm. Or—unique to the US—mentally or physically challenged, requiring special schooling.

As an American with Mexican and Native heritage, Thanksgiving has never been my thing. It never jived with me to celebrate something so inherently anti-me. Fortunately, when you grow up, you can make decisions that resonate with you rather than those dogmatic practices forced upon you by others. For me, that meant marking, with honor, Native American Decimation Day to push back against this fictional narrative of Columbus, the Pilgrims, and Lewis and Clark.

Years of Native and Mexican recipes with the notable absence of turkey and stuffing passed without incident. Until—the third grade. When Son #1 came home, bereft: "We need a turkey!"

"Excuse me?"

"Native American Decimation Day is not normal. I want a REAL Thanksgiving dinner," he said, holding up a construction paper effigy of John Smith.

"Ahh," I said, crouching to meet eye to eye. "But we aren't related to pilgrims. Our ancestors were here first."

"I don't care. Thanksgiving dinner is turkey, potatoes, and pumpkin pie," he wailed.

That was the year I made a traditional baked pumpkin "pie."

It wasn't a big hit. It wasn't normal.

The status quo. The ordinary. The commonplace.

Not normal is *my* norm.

The antiestablishment subpar linguist in me (the only two Cs I earned in my post-grad studies. Hey, we were diagramming sentences and learning about the great vowel shift. Only one of those topics interested me) loves to parse the value of denotation and connotation. One is textbook, and one contains multitudes.

Definitions. Connotations. Languages. Dialects. Standard. Colloquial. All of these things are dynamic. Latin is dead. And rightly so. The list of indigenous languages becoming extinct is lamentably long. When we look at the history of humanity, one of the few constants besides fear of the Other is that there is no normal. The majority wraps itself up in a blanket of normalcy to feel safe and secure, while the rest of us know that's the greatest fiction of all. *Normal* is an attempt to maintain power.

Sir Francis Bacon. Thomas Jefferson. Dr. Seuss. LeVar Burton. Betty White. Not a disparate list of names. Instead, a collection of people devoted to a differing, complex notion: Knowledge Is Power. Since it's a simple idea with intricate underpinning—no shade to the *Reading Rainbow*—I'm inclined to turn to Michel Foucault. He qualified this power-knowledge relationship with correctness. Having the right kind of knowledge becomes an exercise of power. This relationship is inherently cyclical and fictional. The more power you have, the more influence and control you have over what is considered the right kind of knowledge. Language is representative of knowledge. Language is also a mechanism of social and cultural norms.

As a literature teacher, I've taught language as alive, fluid, and muddled. *Ain't* is indeed a word. Language is also mired in its own fiction: history, culture, politics, religion, and civilization. We try to strip that fiction away to find some fundamental truth. We dig for any innate significance. A table is still a table if we remove its name. It still has a purpose and utility. We can still pile coupons, stray pens, junk mail, and random flotsam on it. We can still gather around it. Family. Friends. Games. Meals. Homework.

The labeling of things doesn't imbue them with meaning. Language equaling discourse equaling communication isn't the complete formula. Foucault argued that discourse wasn't simply a method of communicating meaning. Discourse is a way of thinking, feeling, and speaking: a way of interfacing that is institutionalized and defines certain realities. That being said, Foucault argued that the object carries intrinsic meaning outside the naming. However, using language as a social construct means words can become weaponized as tools of conformity. Bossy. Bitch. Wetback. Uncouth. Feminazi.

We all have our lists.

Language becomes a tool of social and cultural majorities to subvert and subjugate ideas outside the generally accepted norms. Cultural norms aren't standardized across society. They aren't even consistent across neighborhoods—let alone countries, states, regions, or religions. And while we may not consciously define our identity based on commonly accepted mores, culture influences how we think and feel. We orient our collective and independent identities by the social and cultural constellations surrounding us.

We may point our ship toward *terra ignota*, but those contrived and oppressive expectations spur us forward. Beyond. Clear of. Free of.

Those of us existing outside the boundaries are considered banished to the fringes of society. THEY don't understand we've always been there. Not banished, but gathered. Narrow-minded, terrified, and so blind to the reality that normal standard routine is a fictional construct, THEY try to use language to shackle us to fear, shame, and ANTI-ness: anti-science, anti-tolerance, anti-other, anti-knowledge.

Language has enslaved humanity.

The writer, the poet, the musician, the artist. Language changes with culture. Changes generationally. With the times. It's a beautiful thing. It can be crafted. Sculpted. Warped. We are living in an extraordinary moment. Many extraordinary moments piled on top of tables that we can use to push past the stagnation. The restriction. The box. We can use language to imagine. To empathize. To manifest.

Language has elevated humanity.

While language can be a tool of the patriarchy, the establishment, and the normative, language can also be the mechanism of rebellion. Of dismantling. Of creation. Of evolution. Michel Foucault thought "every exercise of power depended on the scaffold of knowledge that supports it." The limiting of knowledge, the weaponization of language, and the banning of books, all advance the agendas of some groups while marginalizing others.

More importantly, spheres and groups always exist to undertake the "reconfiguring of power relations in a way that might redress oppressive institutions and practices."[1]

Sir Francis Bacon. Thomas Jefferson. Dr. Seuss. LeVar Burton. Betty White. Questlove. Barack Obama. Betty White. (Yes, again. Admit it, she's a rockstar.) The more you read, the more you know. The more you learn, the better you think critically. Critical thinking involves logic, reasoning, creativity, analysis, empathy, innovation. Magic. Science. Music. Poetry. Mathematics. Art.

We can gather the letters and sentences and lines and paragraphs and quatrains and refrains in the name of language to rise. To revolt. We can eliminate banish obliviate limitations on our potential. Our spirits. Our lives. We can exist for the indeterminate. Look forward, ignore nostalgia. Evolve into and out of. The Past. The Annals. The history. The norms. To embrace the exception.

—*JC Lynne*
Writing Heights Writers Association
Managing Editor, The Writing Bug

[1.] Christopher Pollard, "Explainer: the Ideas of Foucault," *The Conversation*, August 26, 2019, https://theconversation.com/explainer-the-ideas-of-foucault-99758

A Recipe for Normal*

By Sandra McGarry

2½ cups of yesterdays
2 large eggs from the barn before the rooster crowed
1½ cups of moonlight preferably from the Cliffs of Moher
1 tablespoon of laughter
2 minced bulbs of determination
1 vanilla bean whole from a friend in Tahiti

Cream the yesterdays with the moonlight.
Listen to the rooster's crow while mixing.
Fold in the minced bulbs with laughter.
Scrape the vanilla bean pod for seeds.
Blend them so they look like periods
      that lost their sentences.

Pour the ingredients into a pandemic of hope.
Bake until a toothpick exits the batter clean.
Let rest until the sun mutinies.
Cut and wrap slices as you would with kindness.
Write a thank you note to Tahiti.

*For Exceptional Results:
  Read a cookbook.
  Hire a baker. Call Grams.

The Orange Tree

By Katie Lewis

Lottie could still remember the orange from the tree in her grandmother's backyard. She couldn't have been more than four years old, but she remembered watching her grandmother carefully peel the rind back to reveal the white ball nestled inside. Then she'd scraped the white film off with the nail of her thumb, revealing a shade of orange paler than the rind had been.

Lottie remembered watching in fascination as the fruit split easily apart after that. She'd been amazed to realize it didn't need to be cut with a knife. Instead, it came apart in ready-made sections, as if nature had always intended for it to be eaten in easily manageable chunks. As if the whole fruit had been designed especially for her.

Her grandmother set each section on a plate in a small circle. Each piece was about as big as one of Lottie's pudgy fingers, and she remembered her grandmother apologizing for how small the orange was, that the tree had once hung heavy with fruit bigger than softballs. Lottie hadn't known what a softball was, but she understood it was likely much bigger than the little orange that had fit comfortably into her small hand when she'd picked it that morning.

If Lottie had known she was tasting the last orange that tree would ever produce, she might have savored it more. Then again, being only four, maybe not. Even after all these years, though, she could remember the exact feel of it. The sharp tang of citrus in her nose. The way the first segment she popped into her mouth had exploded into juice when she bit down. She'd expected it to be slightly bitter, like the juice she sometimes had with breakfast, but it wasn't. Instead, the taste was bright and joyful on her tongue. Like the feeling of sun on her skin translated into flavor.

Her grandmother had only taken one of the orange segments, leaving the rest for Lottie to enjoy. Maybe she'd known then—known that she'd had the privilege of eating oranges for most of her life while her granddaughter would only get this one chance at a memory. Lottie never thought to ask her before she died.

Grandmother's tree never produced another orange. Hers wasn't the only one, either. In the years that followed, the round fruits became scarcer and scarcer in grocery stores and farmer's market stalls. The scant offerings that did show up grew steadily smaller and more bitter. The few times Lottie's mother tried to buy her oranges in those years, Lottie always spit them out in disgust. The sunshine flavor was gone, replaced with something overcast and angry.

Oranges as a species of fruit were officially declared extinct when Lottie was seven.

The loss of such a staple fruit was hard for many to accept. Orange artificial flavoring still existed, and a sudden tide of candies and baked goods and even liquid medication—all orange flavored—arose almost as a backlash to the loss of the original fruit. Every now and then, when her parents put on the news in the evenings, Lottie would hear a story about attempts to grow new orange trees in greenhouses across the world. It always seemed that something went wrong, however. The nutrients in the soil weren't right or the atmosphere of the greenhouse wasn't humid enough or the blossoms weren't pollinated correctly to produce any fruit. The orange simply refused any attempts at resurrection.

Whenever Lottie heard these stories, she thought of her grandmother's tree. As far as she knew, her grandmother had never done anything special for it, and it had always produced more oranges than anyone knew what to do with—until it had simply stopped. Lottie found it strange to imagine scientists in white suits scrambling to try to reproduce what had once happened all on its own in her grandmother's backyard.

Time passed and the global mourning of the orange began to recede. The list of extinct fruit grew, and people moved on to worship other lost produce with the same explosion of artificial flavoring that had followed the passing of the orange. It became a trend, like the changes in fashion from year to year. Lottie didn't really mind, although the cherry year would live in her mind as the most grotesque year of her life. She had never cared for cherry in the first place, and an entire Halloween bag of cherry-themed candies was enough to firmly put her off cherries for the rest of her life.

Life went on. Older generations lamented the extra vitamins being added to just about any processed food of any kind, even things like potato chips and candy, in an attempt to compensate for a virtually produce-free diet. Every year, Lottie's history teachers would set aside a week to focus on how the American diet had so drastically changed. Sometimes the science teachers joined in for a double whammy. Lottie and her classmates generally agreed that their efforts were more depressing than anything else. Most of them had never even tasted the fruits and vegetables that were "gone" now. Just because the grown-ups couldn't accept change, that didn't mean Lottie and her classmates should have to console them.

Privately, though, Lottie never really forgot about that last orange. Every now and then she'd try to chase down the flavor again, trying juices or sodas or suckers or artificial marmalade. None of it was right, though. The taste was... overwhelmingly bright. The orange in her memories had a softness to it, a tang to temper the sweet. The imitations were just all sweetness. No balance. She didn't hate them exactly, not like the cherry ones, but it wasn't the same.

Lottie's grandmother had baked with her when she was small. Lottie rarely did more than drag a wooden spoon through a bowl of dough, but they still did it together. As a result, she'd inherited all of her grandmother's recipes and kitchen gadgets and shelf-stable ingredients. All of them were placed in a plastic tub in the basement somewhere. Lottie forgot all about them, until high school.

Junior year brought the curse of chemistry. Memorizing the periodic table was a struggle, and Lottie generally disliked the teacher for his seeming inability to explain why certain elements acted the way they did. In fact, she was thoroughly unimpressed with the entire thing and resigned herself to slogging her way through the class as best she could.

Then came their first hands-on experiment.

The assignment was simple enough. Mix four pipettes together and record the results. Counting out droplets, Lottie was suddenly reminded of measuring vanilla extract into a teaspoon for her grandmother's cookies. Just like that, it clicked. Chemistry was simply a different form of baking. Lottie's opinion of the class changed rather drastically after that.

The end of high school was a tense time for Lottie. Her father mistook her interest in chemistry and pushed for her to focus her college studies on that. Women were desirable in the STEM field and she'd surely land a good job, making good money. He utterly ignored the fact that the chemistry class had led Lottie to open the dust-covered tub in the basement containing her inheritance. The fact that she'd spent almost every Saturday for a year experimenting with her grandmother's recipes. The fact that she had now been unofficially appointed as the one solely responsible for any and all desserts at holidays and family gatherings.

Culinary school wasn't an option in her father's mind. It was, however, the only option in Lottie's. Their fights sometimes reached the point of screaming matches, but Lottie was every bit as stubborn as the oranges that refused to grow even in the most perfect and controlled conditions. Her father wore himself out before too long and washed his hands of the situation in disgust. Even at seventeen, Lottie knew that he'd never fully forgive her for this transgression. He would always lament the path not taken, but it was her path to choose, not his. And she wouldn't lament it for a second.

Her resolve was only strengthened by her first full day of classes at the culinary institute. The campus looked just like many of the other "traditional" colleges she'd toured with her parents. They even had dorms. Lottie was living the same life as most of her other classmates who had gone on to college, her school was just more specialized. Her life felt strange and familiar all at once, like her memory of sweet orange segments bursting on her tongue.

Lottie threw herself into her studies. She'd learned from her own home experiments with her grandmother's recipes that the culinary landscape had changed considerably in her own short lifetime. Many ingredients that were called for in older recipes either didn't exist anymore or needed to be emulated through artificial means. Not only that, but FDA regulations now required certain additives—usually vitamins—in restaurant-level cooking.

At first, Lottie feared that her instructors would take the same brooding and resentful approach to these challenges as her history and science teachers had for the past decade. Instead, Lottie soon discovered that the culinary world was more interested in solving problems in the most creative way possible than dwelling on them. Had vanilla extract grown prohibitively expensive due to the decline of vanilla bean harvests? Double the amount and use vanilla essence. Or, even better, experiment with almond extract and find other ingredients to adjust the flavor.

After her first semester, Lottie found she'd been mistaken. Baking wasn't chemistry. It was alchemy.

Of course, fresh produce and natural ingredients were used whenever possible, but Lottie's instructors were also realistic, both in terms of what was available on the open market and what was feasible on a budget. An expensive restaurant or high-end bakery might be able to source as many non-processed ingredients as possible, but for many in the food industry, that simply wouldn't be possible all the time. Humans were adaptable, though, and the fact was that the people who truly cared about all-natural ingredients sought out the more expensive venues that carried them. The general public, on the other hand, was concerned chiefly with taste first and ingredients second. That might not have been the case thirty or even twenty years ago, but it was the world they lived in now, and most people had grown to accept it as a fact of nature.

Lottie worked hard in culinary school. Someday she hoped to open a bakery of her very own, but for now she had to learn all aspects of cooking before she could specialize as a pastry chef. That fact annoyed her at times, but coming out of school with a well-rounded education would be for the best. Her first job as a line chef was far from glamorous, but it was work all the same.

Every now and then, Lottie would look for any updates about the oranges. Some greenhouses in South America were apparently having luck with apples and pears and peaches. Cherries seemed to be more hit or miss. And every orange tree blossomed but never bore. No one could seem to explain it. Other citrus fruits could be coaxed back into existence in laboratories, even if the lemons were small and definitely more sour than Lottie seemed to remember. But no one ever had any luck with oranges.

Lottie split her days between her schooling and working as a kitchen porter in the evenings. She didn't have much time to spend with friends, but then again none of them had the money to do much besides gather once or twice a month on the odd day they could all manage to get off and pass out in the host's living room like they were at a middle school sleepover. It was a hectic sort of life, but one that felt invigorating all the same. All of Lottie's friends these days were fellow culinary classmates. They were all chasing the same dream. Now and then someone would switch to IT work or get married and move away, but a core group formed after a particularly grueling pastry course led by an instructor who spoke more French than English. That experience made them friends for life.

When Lottie was finally granted her pastry chef internship, her grandmother's house became her own. Her mother had never had the heart to sell it. The house had seen various renters since her grandmother's death but had stood empty for the past several years. One could touch either wall of the tiny afterthought of a kitchen if they stretched their arms out, but it was still essentially a free house. Lottie's mother only asked that she pay for utilities.

The kitchen turned out to be less of an issue than Lottie originally suspected. The main counter was on a hinge that folded down against the wall, allowing for more space when necessary. Lottie hadn't understood the purpose of the second oven in the basement until she spent her first sweltering summer in the house. She quickly learned that unless she wanted the entire main floor to be as hot as the cookies she was baking, the oven in the kitchen was only to be used in the winter.

The house was small and odd, but it had three bedrooms and two full bathrooms. Lottie went through several roommates in the first few years she owned the house: usually whoever her current girlfriend was and one other, leaving the last room open as a guest room. The house quickly became the central hub for their infrequent parties.

Every spring, the tree in the backyard blossomed and Lottie would watch it all summer through the kitchen window, searching the branches for even a hint of orange spheres. A few times she saw a swelling green ball that would surely ripen into an orange, but they always either dried up or were eaten by birds within a matter of days. Even so, she kept her eye on the tree.

The pastry chef internship didn't immediately lead to a bakery job as Lottie had hoped, but it was a stepping stone nonetheless. She knew what it took to run a full-scale bakery now, and slowly she began writing up plans and doing her best to estimate budgets in an old journal. One night her current girlfriend, Morgan, caught her at it and offered to help. Morgan was a few years older, having decided to attend the culinary institute after double-majoring in hospitality and business at a more traditional university. For the most part, Lottie's estimates weren't too far off, but Morgan helped correct some of the wilder guesses.

And just like that, Lottie had a business plan. One night over sips of imitation wine, they put the finishing touches on what Lottie would need financially to get a business loan for her own bakery. Suddenly, she had a tangible goal and, after graduating from the culinary institute in the spring, Lottie threw herself into her work twice as hard as before to save up the necessary funds.

Morgan lasted longer than any other relationship Lottie had ever had. She didn't begrudge Lottie the hours she worked or accuse Lottie of putting her second. In truth, she seemed just as invested in Lottie's dream bakery as Lottie was herself. So much so, in fact, that one night Morgan took Lottie to a restaurant far fancier than anything either of them were used to for dinner. Lottie was sure Morgan was going to propose, and she did, in a way. Rather than proposing marriage, though, it was a business proposal that Morgan offered over the dairy-free cheesecake they had for dessert. She would cover half the initial investment and offer her excellent credit score for the business loan in exchange for being a full partner. Morgan was better at working with meat than baking, but she had a mind for business and that was the piece Lottie was missing.

Lottie could bake and Morgan would handle the finances and together they could accomplish what neither could alone. After their business loan was approved, Lottie was the one who picked out a ring and made the other sort of proposal.

The two of them lived alone in Lottie's grandmother's house after that. They spent long evenings in the dining room, going over the spaces available for rent downtown and trying to decide on what was both within budget and in a prime location. At last, they settled on a spot and after a bit of financial shuffling, they had their bakery.

The orange tree in the backyard was blossoming when they closed on the space. There were more flowers on it than Lottie had ever seen before. Lottie took it as a sign and named her bakery The Orange Tree. Morgan didn't quite get it—she'd never tasted a real orange in her life—but she didn't fight it either. According to her, trees generally made good logos, and the name was unique enough to stick in people's minds.

Lottie didn't pay her usual attention to the orange tree that summer. She and Morgan were too busy getting the space ready to open: walls to repaint, tile to replace, counters to seal, a long list of equipment to buy or rent, and a thousand other miscellaneous chores that needed completing before the bakery could open. They barely even saw the house except to shower and collapse into bed.

So, it wasn't until everything was almost ready in midsummer that they decided to give themselves a well-earned Sunday off. Lottie was sitting in front of the television, her mind seven miles away on her bakery and all the things she still needed to do before the grand opening, when Morgan suddenly screamed from the kitchen.

"Holy shit. Holy shit! Lottie! Get in here!" Morgan shouted. Lottie was up and sprinting, her heart in her throat. Was there a mouse? Or a spider? Or a moth? When she got to the kitchen, however, Morgan wasn't cowering. Instead she was staring out the kitchen window with her mouth open. She raised one hand, still gripping the neck of a sweating beer bottle, and pointed at something out the window. Lottie had to almost put her head on Morgan's shoulder to see. When she did, her entire body froze.

The branches of the tree in the backyard were bowing towards the ground in the fading evening light. Great round fruits were visible between the leaves, twinkling like a hundred tiny suns.

"No way..." Lottie whispered. Without another word she turned and ran barefoot out of the side door, rushing through the prickly grass straight up to the tree for a closer look. Most of the oranges had fully come into their color, though a few were still green around the stem. They were big, too. Big enough to fill Lottie's palm the same way the smaller offering from more than twenty years ago had done. Muscle memory took over and Lottie twisted her wrist, pulling the ripe fruit free of the tree as her grandmother had demonstrated so long ago.

"Wait," Morgan said, just as Lottie was digging her thumbnail into the rind. "It might be poisonous. People have gone to the hospital because of home gardens."

"Just one," Lottie said, carefully working the skin off her prize now. "We'll split it. Even if we get sick, it can't be worse than that time we got food poisoning from the Greek place." Morgan groaned, either at Lottie's obstinance or at the memory of two days of intense misery. Either way, though, she came closer to peer over Lottie's shoulder.

"Fine," Morgan said at last. "But if it tastes weird, spit it out. I mean it, Lottie."

"I'm not an idiot," Lottie grunted, frowning as part of the peel fell into the grass. She'd been trying to get it all in one long strip like her grandmother had done. "These are called Valencia oranges, I think," she added, picking at the rind to pull it up and keep going. "They're supposed to be sweeter. Or I remember it being sweet, anyway."

"Weird," Morgan muttered, taking a swig of her beer.

It took longer than Lottie thought it would, but at last she freed the orange from its peel. There was a lot of white pulpy film, and she started to scrape it off with her fingernails before she grew too impatient and found a crease between segments where she could start to pull the fruit apart.

"Careful, don't squish it," Morgan chided. Lottie ignored her. The fruit split in half easily enough and Lottie handed over one half, examining her own. They exchanged a glance before Morgan set down her beer and they each pulled a single segment free. It looked just like Lottie remembered, lighter in color than the rind but still vibrant.

"On the count of three?" Morgan asked, glancing around at the neighboring houses as if she expected someone to run out and stop them. Lottie knocked her segment against Morgan's in an approximation of a toast.

"One," Lottie said.

"Two," Morgan said.

"Three!" they said together.

Lottie threw caution to the wind and popped the entire piece into her mouth. The white pulp she'd left on was bitter on her tongue, but the moment she bit down her mouth was flooded with liquid sunshine. The taste was just as sweet as she remembered, not cloying like the artificial flavorings. And at the end came the balance of tang she remembered.

"Holy shit," Morgan said again. She'd only taken a bite of her own piece and now she hurried to get the rest in her mouth before the precious juice dripped onto her fingers. "Is it . . . supposed to taste like this?" she asked, genuinely curious. "It's so *good*."

"Yeah," Lottie said, turning to beam up at the tree. "It's supposed to taste like this."

They ate the rest of the orange in the dying light. The only sound that passed between them was the occasional groan of satisfaction when they bit into another piece. When they were done, both of them had to resist the urge to pick as many oranges as they could. It was growing too dark to be sure which ones were ripe any longer, and neither wanted to risk ruining one by picking it too early.

They came to two mutual decisions that night without even needing to discuss them with one another. The first: provided that neither of them got sick from the orange they'd shared, they would absolutely be incorporating the oranges in the grand opening spread Lottie had been planning for the bakery. The second: there would be no advertisement about it whatsoever. The sudden harvest was most likely a fluke. The tree hadn't produced oranges in over two decades. Not even scientists had been able to make oranges in that time. And they both knew that those selfsame scientists would dig the tree up and cart it away if they knew about it, and neither of them wanted that.

Two days later, when neither of them had shown any signs of illness, Lottie and Morgan carried every bucket, basket, and bowl they could find out into the backyard to pick as much of the ripe fruit as they could. They sorted the "ugly" ones to keep for themselves and carted the rest to the bakery.

Several oranges were set aside to be candied. They were sliced and simmered in sugar and set out on racks to dry. Once Lottie was convinced she had enough slices, she set to work on the rest of the oranges.

After a thorough washing, a majority of the remaining oranges were zested until they had no color left at all, reduced to balls of white pulp. Then Lottie considered the possibility that she'd never come across natural orange zest again and grated the rest of them as well.

With that task completed, Lottie plucked out one orange for each of the fifteen cakes she intended to make and juiced the rest. Lottie used the metal instrument she'd inherited from her grandmother. The juicing was murder on her arms and shoulders, leaving them feeling like limp noodles by the end of the day. In the end, though, she filled a few gallon jugs with fresh-squeezed orange juice. She locked up that night with a plan already in place for the mass assembly that would happen the next day, two days ahead of the grand opening.

Lottie arrived bright and early with the index cards of her grandmother's orange cake recipe in her hands. She laid them out in a corner for easy reference and put on her apron.

First came the sponge cakes, simple enough to make, though a few ingredients had to be substituted these days. Each batch of batter received a helping of the orange zest mixed in before they were set to bake. Lottie watched them through the glass door, paranoid of allowing them to fall or burn.

Once the cakes had finished and cooled, the real fun began. Dairy-replacement heavy cream was whipped with another generous helping of orange zest. While it chilled, Lottie leveled each sponge cake with a careful eye. Then it was time to fire up the stove and simmer a syrup that was equal parts orange juice and cognac with sugar. The syrup was brushed liberally onto the sponge cakes to add flavor and keep them moist.

The next part was trickiest only because it had the most moving parts. Each bottom cake was topped with an even spread of the chilled whipped cream. Lottie chopped the oranges she'd set aside and added the pieces, one orange per cake, coating them with more cream. Finally, the top cakes were settled into place and the creation could be transferred to the fridge to chill.

From there, each cake had to be treated individually, which was why Lottie had allotted the entire day to this project alone. She fired up a clean stand mixer to make a buttercream frosting, the only part of her grandmother's recipe that didn't need to be altered—save for the fact that Lottie had to use orange essence instead of orange extract. The taste should be the same, though. And, indeed, it came out not too cloying, with only the barest hint of orange.

Lottie took her time with each cake. Adding a single layer of icing one at a time and setting no less than three timers at any given moment to ensure they all had ample time for the base layer to chill and harden. Once she'd gone through them all once, she pulled them out again one by one to finish the icing.

Last of all, Lottie fired up the stove again to make a glaze from the orange juice she'd squeezed yesterday, mixed with cornstarch and sugar. The glaze was meant to offset the sweetness of the buttercream, so she was light with the sugar. Once the first pot was done, it went into the chiller to cool and she started on another.

From that point on, Lottie was a machine. Each cake received eight equal swirls piped on top. After that, she cut the candied orange slices in half and lined the bottom of the cake with them. Fourths of the candied oranges were arranged to stand upright in the piped swirls and garnished with mint for a splash of green. Finally, the cooled glaze was spooned over the top, filled with more orange zest and chopped strips of candied orange. Only then was each finished cake put back into the cooler.

Fifteen cakes were made in all, and Lottie honestly would have left without cleaning up if Morgan hadn't shown up around dinner time to help. There wasn't any part of Lottie's body that didn't hurt by the end, but she'd done it. And the town was in for the shock of its life.

The next day was split between decorating and making a variety of cookies, brownies, cupcakes, and generally much more mundane baked goods. Lottie wasn't up for much else, and besides, it wouldn't do to overshadow the main attraction.

When The Orange Tree opened, about forty-five harrowing minutes passed before the first customer arrived. She was an older woman, in her sixties or early seventies.

"Welcome!" Morgan almost pounced on her, only staying behind the counter because Lottie was fast enough to grab her apron strings. "Have a slice of Orange Tree Cake—on the house!" She gestured at one of the cakes they had set out for display while Lottie handed over a paper plate with a pre-cut slice. She and Morgan had eaten their own slices this morning, nearly in tears, but Lottie still watched the woman's face closely. The woman's eyes slipped closed at the first bite, only to snap open again in shock.

"Oh! Oh my!" she gasped, gaping at them both. "But . . . this really *does* taste like orange. I haven't had oranges in y*ears*! How . . . ?"

"Secret recipe!" Morgan was quick to reply. Lottie only smiled, understanding now the joy and wonder her grandmother must have seen in her own face when she'd eaten that first-and-almost-last orange, all those years ago.

Sitting in poetry class...

By Megan E. Freeman

Sitting in poetry class, I am an egg grief cracks open and separates into two bowls, my whites whipped stiff with sorrow at the certain fact that you will die. Or I will. And we will not be together so I can tell you about the pieces of shell that fall into the batter.

But in the other bowl, my yolk rests whole and glowing, knowing, at least, that death has not come today, and there is still time to call and tell you all about it.

Elegy for a Hawthorne

By Janet Kamnikar

In this neighborhood of big old trees,
ours the last house built on the block,
the hawthorne we planted that first summer
never matched those giants,
but stayed proportional
to our postage-stamp front yard.
It knew its place.

It gave us twenty-one years
of May blossom,
a bridesmaid's bouquet to cherish;
little red berries in the fall;
and slender bare December branches
that proved a perfect framework
for tiny Christmas lights.

But last year we watched it
wither. A March snowstorm
took a heavy toll in broken limbs.
In April it sprouted
leaves already yellowed: fire blight,
two different tree men said,
nothing to be done.

It took you two days
and a borrowed power saw
to cut it down;
I snapped photos, the camera lens
blurred by tears.
The daylilies that frilled
around its base
now hide the small, flat stump.

The emptiness is a presence,
though a thin sprite of a cherry tree
anchors itself in a new spot
in the green lawn,
our adopted child
whose full growth
we will not see.

aka Estate Sale

By Celia Turner

Nowhere to be found is the word yard,
although the grass is trampled to dirt.
In the basement her reading glasses lie
as if she had just set them down
by the sewing machine and stepped
next door for a cup of coffee
instead of eternity. Photo album
in steamer trunk of long-dead relatives—
so much for ancestry.com.
Below, hand-sewn embroidered quilt
protected from sun's destructive rays.
Procession of strangers pall-bearing possessions.
Well-used instruments in velvet-lined cases
sit poised for final fingering.

Somewhere relatives are vacationing
in Europe or in their second home in Vail
saying *send me the money*.

Cleave

By Celia Turner

Write me a poem about this nest,
she says, hoping for beauty,
magic and mystery

but instead of turquoise eggs,
there is no small coincidence
we don't hear the call of robins,

that the nest was blown down,
empty, old, that soon the robin
may not find a mate,

that it may be a reminiscence
when there were birds,
that bleakness rests heavily upon us.

The Incredible, Uncanny Interview!

By David E. Sharp

Elliot Finnes took slow, deep breaths and tried to slow his heart rate as he sat on the uncomfortable office bench. The rapid keystrokes of the intern at the reception desk worked against his calming measures. Elliot's pulse quickened as if to sync with the sound.

"They're ready for you, Mr. Finnes," said the intern with a professional nod, then he returned to his typing. The man's conservative blazer and creased slacks over a brightly colored spandex suit would have been an odd combination anywhere but a semiformal Halloween party, a board meeting of yoga instructors, or within the walls of this building.

Elliot rose from his bench. His stomach dropped to his toes. He hadn't endured nerves this shaky since his roommate made him ask Rachel Devereaux to dinner after Elliot lost a bet. He sucked in a lungful of air and tightened his grip on his resume. He approached the nine-foot titanium double doors.

"Allow me," said the intern, placing two fingers on his forehead and glancing at the doors. The doors opened with a loud metallic scrape.

"Thank you." Elliot stepped through the threshold into a massive room with a vaulted ceiling and glass wall that displayed a view of the bustling city twenty-seven stories below. In the center of the room, three figures sat on the far side of a large table. Three figures Elliot had never believed he would see in the flesh.

On the left, a petite woman in a lavender and gold leotard with filigree in the style of ancient Greece adjusted her spectacles and rifled through a stack of papers.

"Herculisa," whispered Elliot to himself.

On the right, a muscular man in a black cape and a mask that made him look like an angry owl leaned on one elbow and stared at his own gauntlet-clad fist with grim intensity. Elliot noticed cufflinks arranged on the gauntlets to give them a more business-like feel.

"The Brood Knight," said Elliot to no one.

Between them sat the man himself, dressed in his trademark blue and red spandex suit, but with the addition of a maroon necktie. He furrowed his brow at a pen he repeatedly clicked in his hand, though it did not seem to work. The ink tip refused to emerge.

Elliot stopped short and gasped. "Justice Guy."

He had seen their pictures in all the newsfeeds. Followed their careers. He remembered when they had taken down Admiral Abominable and his sea monsters. Forget Rachel Devereaux! This was the most nervous Elliot had ever been. The pictures did nothing to convey what it felt like to be in the presence of these incredible heroes with their intense eyes, their perfectly cleft chins, and their inexplicable love of spandex.

Justice Guy raised a hand toward him. "Be with you in just a moment. Thank you for your patience." He turned to Herculisa and gestured at the pen. "Why do these things always break?"

"Let me try." Herculisa snatched the pen from Justice Guy's grip and gave it a few clicks. It crumpled in her hand. "Whoops! Well, it's definitely broken now."

Justice Guy waved it off. "I'll get another." He cupped his mouth with one hand and called out, "Intern Boy! I'm going to need a new pen."

"On it, sir," came the intern's voice from the receiving room at Elliot's back. Moments later, a shiny new pen levitated across the room, flew over Elliot's shoulder, and landed in Justice Guy's waiting hand.

Justice Guy gave it a click and a subsequent approving nod. "That will do." He looked up at Elliot and gestured to a chair across the table. "Please, have a seat, Mr. Finnes."

Elliot pulled the chair out and placed himself upon it, directly in the nexus of three super-powered gazes. He gave each of them a shaky nod and said, "Hello. Thank you for seeing me." He placed his resume on the table and noticed the sweat stains where he had been holding it. Elliot frowned at the soiled paper, betrayed by the moisture from his hands. He grimaced and slid the resume across the table.

Justice Guy picked it up, obviously avoiding the sweaty spots, and ran his eyes over it. "Yes, yes. Nice GPA. Completed culinary school. Average typing speed."

"What does it say about his origin story?" asked The Brood Knight.

"My what?" said Elliot.

"The pain from your past," said The Brood Knight. "What you contemplate when you stand on the roof of skyscrapers. Who twisted you into the vengeful agent of violent justice you are today? WHO MURDERED YOUR PARENTS, FINNES?"

"Wh-What?" Elliot stammered, trying to form a response. "No-Nobody. Nobody murdered them. My dad works for the water company, and my mom manages a boutique in an outlet mall."

"A friend then? A lover? Someone close to you died in your arms, pleading to you through choked gasps while you stood there hopeless. *'Why, Elliot? Why didn't you save me?'* And now you wander the night, saving everyone but the one person who ever really mattered. The one person who is lost to you forever. And every day you become more a stranger to yourself until you wonder: Is Elliot Finnes even real anymore? Was he ever real? Is it something like that?"

Elliot fell out of his chair. From the floor, he met the Brood Knight's terrifying gaze. "No! Never! Nothing like that. Ever!"

"Don't play games with me, Finnes!" The Brood Knight rose and slammed his fist on the table. "I will find the truth!"

Justice Guy cleared his throat. "Let's, uh . . . let's get back to the resume."

The Brood Knight sat down. Elliot rose from the floor and replaced the fallen chair a little closer to Herculisa's side of the table. Then he took a seat.

Justice Guy glanced at the paper in his hands. His eyes grew wide. "Ooh! It says here you owned a food truck."

"Ooh!" echoed Herculisa.

Justice Guy lowered the resume. "What kind of food truck?"

"Baked potatoes. Like with a lot of toppings and stuff."

Herculisa's stomach growled. It was loud enough to echo in the giant space. "Sorry," she said. "I haven't had lunch yet, and my super-strength demands a heavy calorie intake."

Justice Guy threw back his head and laughed. "As tiny as she is, you wouldn't believe the damage she can do to a buffet table."

Herculisa fired a glare at her colleague. It was fortunate, thought Elliot, that she did not have laser eyes.

Justice Guy composed himself and set the resume down. "So tell me, Mr. Finnes. Why do you want to be a Hero?"

Elliot shrugged. "I guess I just needed a change."

The Brood Knight leaned forward, holding Elliot in his murderous eyes. "You just needed a change?" His voice was gravelly and cold. "You're bored with your life, so you want to take on the most dangerous criminals on the planet, endure torture, and protect the city with your own blood and pain, is that it?"

Elliot flinched. "No! I mean, I'm not crazy about the torture. Or the blood and pain stuff."

"Then what is it?" asked The Brood Knight.

"Well," said Elliot. "I just ended a long hospital stay following an accident that destroyed my food truck. I lost everything. It gave me plenty of time to think."

"What did you think about?" asked Herculisa.

"Life is so short," said Elliot. "People always say it can end at any moment, but getting such a close look at my own mortality really drove the point home. Made me ask the hard questions. I don't want to waste my life. I want to make a difference."

"And by making a difference, you mean you would like to go toe-to-toe with Dr. Diablo," said Justice Guy, balling up his fists and pantomiming a boxing match.

"Or The Atomic Brute," added Herculisa.

"Or The Amputator," said The Brood Knight.

Elliot sweated through his shirt. "I don't think I am ready for any of those criminals. Maybe I can start with a few of the easier ones. Do you have any serial embezzlers?"

Justice Guy snorted, Herculisa let out a long breath, and The Brood Knight brooded. "Embezzlers?" said Justice Guy, furrowing his brow and holding Elliot in a gaze of superpowered derision. "What do you think we are? Super accountants? Did you even *look* at the job description?"

Herculisa produced a paper from her stack and read aloud. "Wanted. Daring do-gooder with steely nerves and even steelier muscles. Job duties include, but are not limited to: punching bad guys, kicking bad guys, throwing bad guys into other bad guys, disarming bombs at the last second, infiltrating enemy compounds, surveying the city from rooftops, posing for photo ops, and spouting pithy one-liners. Must be able to lift and carry 800 lbs. Superhuman abilities preferred."

"Thank you, Herculisa." Justice Guy tapped his fingers on the surface of the table. "Are you planning to punch or kick some embezzlers, Mr. Finnes?"

Elliot sighed. "I admit I'm not very good at the punching or kicking. Or that part about throwing bad guys into other bad guys."

"Then why do you want to be a Hero?" asked Herculisa. She perched her spectacles on the tip of her nose and stared at him.

"It's the last part." Elliot pointed at the job description in her hand. "The part about superhuman abilities. I have one of those."

Justice Guy perked up and cleared his throat. "You? *You* have a superhuman ability?"

Elliot nodded. "Ever since I woke up at the hospital. You see, my accident was no ordinary accident. A van transporting chemicals from a top-secret laboratory ran a stop sign and T-boned me in an intersection. The chemicals and all the ingredients from my food truck came together and altered my genetic code."

Justice Guy nodded and a grin spread across his face. "Excellent! Yes! *Now* we're getting somewhere. Tell me more about these powers of yours."

Elliot smiled for the first time since he set foot in this building. "I can make any food taste like any other food."

The three Heroes stared in silence. It was excruciating. At length, Justice Guy said, "That's it?"

Elliot nodded. "I mean, I can make ice cream taste like tacos. Or I can make something bland taste like a juicy steak. Or I could make anything taste like bacon. Like, *everything* taste like bacon."

"That'll be handy," said The Brood Knight, a hint of sarcasm in his voice. "While you sit in a dark closet, tied to a chair, waiting for Dr. Diablo to take bids on your vital organs—at least the greasy gag in your mouth will taste like salty breakfast meats." The Brood Knight slammed his palms against the surface of the table. "Don't waste our time, Finnes!"

Justice Guy frowned. "I'm afraid he's right, Mr. Finnes. I don't see how changing the taste of food is going to stop a bank robbery. Or disarm a doomsday device."

Elliot's throat tightened up. "I thought it could be handy for espionage. I could hide the taste of poisons or make the bad guys think their food has gone bad or something."

Justice Guy clicked his tongue. "We're not assassins, Mr. Finnes. We don't use poisons. We use muscles and combat prowess and laser beams."

"Right." Elliot gripped the edge of the table. "I'm so stupid. I should have realized I would never fit in with all of you. I just thought this is what you do when you develop superhuman abilities. You know? Make the world a better place."

Justice Guy folded the resume and set it aside. "Making the world a better place is what *I* do when I develop superhuman abilities. I don't know if that's what *you* do, Mr. Finnes. Sorry."

"No offense, Mr. Finnes," said Herculisa. She plucked up the resume, unfolded it, and held it in front of her eyes. "With these qualifications, I just worry you would become a liability on the battlefield, and we can't always be rescuing you."

"Right!" said Justice Guy, heaving a massive sigh. "We have *enough* people to rescue as it is. You wouldn't *believe* the stupid things people do that end with us rescuing them." Elliot had never thought Justice Guy would consider rescues such a chore.

Herculisa gasped at the resume in her hands. "Hang on a minute! This address. I've seen it before."

The Brood Knight snatched the paper from her hands and scrutinized it. "I recognize it too! Check the database."

"Already on it." Herculisa whipped out a phone and began rapidly tapping the screen.

Elliot felt an icy sensation crawl across his skin. He was a fool to think this would go unnoticed. He wondered, if he abandoned the interview now and made for the door, could he escape this awful room before they caught up to him with their superhuman speed?

Herculisa gasped again, staring at her phone. "I was right. This is the address of Professor Nebula. One of the archest of all our archnemeses! Does he *live* with you?"

Elliot swallowed traces of moisture into his dry throat. "Professor Nebula is, uh, my roommate."

Justice Guy stood, his chair scraping the floor as he rose. "How dare you even walk into this building if you're in cahoots with Professor Nebula! We could never associate with such a diabolical fiend or any of his cronies." He spat the word *cronies* with vile contempt.

"It's not like that," said Elliot quickly. "We're not in cahoots. I mean, outside of having a schedule for whose day it is to do the dishes. And I'm not a crony. That's insulting!"

"Then why do you live with him?" asked The Brood Knight.

Elliot held his palms out. "He answered an ad I posted. I mean, come on! Rent is expensive! I needed a roommate with good hygiene, and he needed a place after you all wrecked his satellite base last summer. I mean, throwing it into the sun was overkill, right? You have to admit!"

"I have to admit nothing!" Herculisa huffed. "How can you even live with such scum?"

"Professor Nebula is a good roommate," said Elliot. "He pays his bills on time. He hangs his towels on the drying rack. And we have game nights every Thursday. I knew it could be awkward if I got the position, but we had a talk about boundaries and keeping work at work and home at home. Besides that, he was my ride here. He's literally waiting for me outside."

Justice Guy placed his knuckles on the table. "Let me make sure I understand you. Professor Nebula is . . . here?"

Elliot scooted his chair back and gripped the armrests. "He is."

Justice Guy spoke through clenched teeth, his self-control obviously suspended by a thread. "Get. Out."

Elliot obeyed as quickly as he was able. He darted out of the room, passed Intern Boy who was watching videos on his phone, rode the elevator down twenty-seven floors, and sprinted out of the building.

Professor Nebula sat on a bench with an open paperback in his hand and his black cape draped over the backrest where people couldn't sit on it. He looked up from his book as Elliot approached and smiled. "Elliot! How did it go?"

Elliot shook his head. "Never mind. If that's what it means to be a hero, I don't want it. Abilities or no abilities, I don't care."

Professor Nebula sighed. "I was afraid of that."

"They're such a bunch of condescending jerks! How can anybody *stand* them?"

"I know," said Professor Nebula. "*Believe me.* I know. Ready to get out of here?" He gestured at the eleven-foot-tall walking tank awaiting them where it was double parked in the lot.

"Let's go," said Elliot.

In moments, they had left the entire compound behind them. Elliot watched the world pass through the bulletproof window.

"Want to talk?" asked Professor Nebula.

Elliot ran his fingers through his hair. "I just don't get it. These are the people who are supposed to make the world better? Why are they so awful?"

"Life is funny that way, isn't it?" said Professor Nebula. "Full of little ironies."

"Why is it so hard?"

"Why is what so hard?"

"To do something that matters? To find the place where I can make a difference?"

Professor Nebula honked at the tiny Volvo in front of them whose driver seemed to think the entire city was a school zone. The walking tank's horn had all the subtly of a raging elephant, and the Volvo's tires squealed as it fled into the next lane. "Maybe it isn't as hard as you think, Elliot."

"Then why can't I find it?" asked Elliot. "Why can't I *ever* find it?"

Professor Nebula shrugged. "Maybe you're looking in the wrong places."

Elliot shook his head. "I don't know."

"I do," said Professor Nebula. "Open the glove box, would you?"

"What? Why?"

"Just do it, Elliot."

Elliot opened the glove box. He dug through an array of sinister weapons, a world map with cryptic symbols drawn on it, a couple of undelivered ransom notes composed of letters cut from newspapers and magazines, and a photograph of Professor Nebula's daughter in her graduation gown. "What am I looking for?"

"It's right there beneath the death ray."

"This thing?" Elliot drew a small, folded paper from the clutter and opened it. The words "Volunteers Needed" appeared in large black letters. "What's this?"

"The local soup kitchen is understaffed. I saw that and thought of you. Have you considered how they could cut costs on seasonings if they had you in the kitchen?"

Elliot ran a finger over the words. "Such tastes I could create."

"Look, Elliot. Do you ever find it odd that everyone who develops superhuman abilities has to weaponize them somehow? Won't this make a bigger difference than all that punching and kicking?"

Elliot folded the paper and looked out the window. He clenched his fists and surveyed the passing cityscape with intense determination. "Such tastes I *will* create."

Fakers

By Emily Rodgers-Ramos

The Buddhist monks gather to laugh. Nothing is funny.
Yet they stand together and pretend
to laugh—forcing it out in gusts—until true mirth explodes.

I, too, come from a long line of sacred fakers: the cuttlefish
masquerading as a rock, the butterfly with fierce owl-eyes tattooed
on his back, the blue jay imitating the hawk's cry at the feeder.

The bird pretending to be a tree stump.
The mantis impersonating an orchid.
The possum teaching her children to play dead.

My mother, after regaining consciousness,
twisted in the tractor's auger, repeating
for our sake, It's okay. I'm okay.

Who really feels grateful before picking up
the gratitude journal each evening? And if you
stand like Wonder Woman, feet apart,

hands on hips, chin up, your gaze will
slice steel. You will be fierce with
purpose; you will be Wonder itself.

Give it a try. Say, my hands are always
steady. Say, I am at home in this world. Say,
I belong here.

Art Modeling / Post-Fire Succession

By Charlotte Suttee

How long until the tea.

Stills back into life.

Insects. Breath.

The Teeming.

Can you see the dry.

Grass hailing. Its crackling.

Hope. I strike matches.

Afraid. Life will find a way.

Without me. Today.

I pose naked. At the mercy of.

Charcoal.

Channeling the Vice President

By Warren Jonsten

Once the toothpaste is out of the tube, it is awfully hard to get it back in.
—*H. R. (Bob) Haldeman*

Mike, why? I told you. You didn't listen. My people caught you sprinting through Congressional halls, too old, too slow. Now you're dangling from a tree outside Schumer's window.

And I've got a problem.

They'll blame me for inciting a riot, urging your assassination. What to do? What to do?

Mr. President, install barbed wire around the White House, erect prison tents everywhere, and reinstate instant capital punishment, firing squad at twenty paces.

Mike, yes, perfect!

Take on the role of Supreme Leader, suspend elections, declare Martial Law, nationalize state and local law enforcement.

Marshall Law, beautiful! I need a shiny silver star for my lapel.

Authorize a private militia, one hundred thousand men per state, armed with AR-15s, and make them take an oath.

Magnificent! How do you come up this stuff?

Confiscate all weapons. Don't take the chance with a mob of hysterical extremists.

Of course! Mike, you're the man!

Dissolve Congress, execute their leaders—examples for the people to see.

Why didn't I think of that? I never liked that whore Pelosi anyway.

The court system?—superfluous. Padlock court houses and seize television and radio stations, the web, and newspapers, replace them with Trump's America, the people want to hear from you.

Nice touch! You're amazing.

Same with social media, it's just a place for dissidents anyway.

Impressive! Mike, I should've kept you around longer.

What Matters Most

by Mary Kay Knief

Travel back to Kansas from
craggier places,
or desert lands, and
you see those flat fields
of rippling wheat,
see the farmer
inside a red or green combine,
stereo blaring in headset,
and a new concept
of beauty emerges.

They're gathering the crop—
it pours into the truck
for the trip to the elevator.
Pull the lever, and
the golden grain
falls through the grate
into the ground, later to
be conveyed upward,
into the round, white
prairie skyscraper.

It's a hard living.
For those fathers and sons
with ag degrees from
land grant colleges,
so much depends
on the uncontrollable—
sun, rain, possible hail.

When corporate farmers
come to buy the land,
it is tempting to say, "Yes,
take it, all of it.
We'll move to town,
work as mechanics,
God knows we have experience.
We'll work eight to five,
get a regular paycheck."

They'll say they're glad their next meal
doesn't depend on the weather.
But they'll always watch the sky.

The Conformist

By Carol A. Fichtelman

A man must consider what a rich realm he abdicates when he becomes a conformist.
—*Ralph Waldo Emerson*, Early Lectures: 1838-1842

I am a creature of habit. A conformist. I like to play it safe.

So my Monday begins as expected. I wake up (always a good thing, unless you have a death wish), shower, shave, get dressed, feed the cat, make coffee, gulp down said coffee, then hustle off to work. But not before stuffing smartphone, wallet, keys, and university ID (always, *always*, in that order) in my pants pockets.

As I said, I'm a creature of habit. I stick to my routine.

Normally I walk to work. Rain or shine. Sleet or snow. My apartment's about a mile and a half away from the university where I work, so it's an easy hike. Plus, it looks to be a standard St. Louis spring day: sunny sky, puffy clouds, warm breezy weather that'll become rainy and overcast and cold by early evening. However, today, for whatever reason (call it a whim?), my brain commands me to take the bus. Why not? After all, the bus stop is right smack in front of my apartment building.

So I fish out the university-issued transportation pass squirreled away in my wallet, have my picture-ID-cum-swipe-card ready, and wait alongside my fellow travelers. We seem a common, ordinary bunch. Just your average conventional law-abiding citizens waiting for the bus. Finally it arrives. You know, the standard-issue type. And we board one by one, careful not to jostle one another.

Then the driver shuts the door and we're off. I'm about ready to sit behind the driver so I can exit first, as is my wont, when—for some strange reason I cannot fathom—I start shuffling towards the very back of the bus like a puppet on a string. As though some magnetic force is pulling me back there.

So there I sit. All alone. In the way, way back of the bus.

And then my very ordinary day turns very extraordinary. One minute the bus is whizzing down Wydown Boulevard in St. Louis towards the university, then, in the blink of an eye, it's shooting past the Eiffel Tower.

Yes, *the* Eiffel Tower. The one in Paris. Paris, France.

"Hey, Harry, you're late," grumbles Tom, barely glancing up from his computer screen; he's my immediate boss and barely older than I am. "It's after ten. Schaffner needs this stuff by two, so get your ass in gear."

"Yeah, I hear you. And don't call me Harry. It's Harrison."

"What's with you today? You're lucky your parents didn't name you Yoda."

"For your information, my dad studied computational linguistics at MIT and the Collège de France in Paris. And my mom was no dummy either; she taught French and German here. So shut up about my parents. At least they didn't name me Thomas Isaac Thomas."

"Okay, okay. Sorry. Didn't realize you were so touchy."

Touchy? Of course I'm "touchy" about my parents. Particularly about my father. The guy who'd constantly disappear, then magically reappear, babbling incoherent gibberish about being in all sorts of places. The guy my mom explained was schizophrenic, maybe bipolar, who refused to take his meds. And now me? After my morning bus ride? Am I crazy like my father?

Dumping doubts of my sanity to the back of my brain, I place the black backpack edged in neon-yellow tape beneath my desk and log onto my computer, pulling up Professor Schaffner's files. You've probably heard of the guy. He chairs the university's Physics Department and founded its Quantum Mechanics Lab. Plus he's a disciple of Anton Zeilinger, the acclaimed Austrian physicist and putative father of QM. Schaffner's career has basically mirrored Zeilinger: University of Vienna, Munich, the ILL, MIT, Collège de France, then (unlike Zeilinger) Princeton and now here. Working in good old mainstream St. Louis.

Schaffner's also a demanding, prickly pain-in-the-ass Teutonic taskmaster. But so what? It's just a job. So after stowing the backpack (and brushing off those clingy corkscrew red hairs), I put my nose to the grindstone like a good little worker bee. Checking data. Crunching numbers. You know, the usual conventional boring stuff.

Then it's lunchtime.

Typically Tom and I chow down together in the staff commons. But not today. Today is special. Tom's picking out a diamond engagement ring for his girlfriend, Michelle. You know the type: beautiful, brainy but bossy Asian-American grad student who's earning a doctorate in chemistry yet yearning to settle down, buy a house, have 2.5 kids, then teach at the university level. Tom seems happy, though. Or so he says.

"Hey, Harry, don't forget, I'll be getting back late. Okay? Want to get Michelle the best ring possible. Without breaking the bank, of course."

"What about New York? I thought you were taking a few days off, looking at rings in the Diamond District?"

"Already been there. Anyway, I'm off. Later."

Already been there? How was that possible? Unless...

For some reason, Tom stomps off in the direction of Schaffner's office instead of the exit. And I'm left alone. With this eerie feeling in the pit of my stomach. Like déjà vu all over again, as Yogi Berra would say. Also, I'm feeling flummoxed over what happened (or did it?) on the bus this morning. Maybe a stroll across campus to clear the cobwebs will help...

Yet the fresh air doesn't ease my anxiety. I still feel strange. As if I'm a jellyfish floating in air. And my skin tingles. Weird. Maybe I should call the university mental health hotline?

But my brain screams, *No, don't do it!*

Am I in denial? Or perhaps I'm waiting for the other proverbial shoe to drop. Or maybe I'm just hungry.

I duck into the student union and grab some grub before heading back to the Physics Department. However, there are way too many people yakking it up in the staff commons for me to think straight—after all, it's twelve thirty, height of the typical worker's lunchtime—so I decide to consume my sandwich at my desk. Try and puzzle this problem out in peace and quiet. Relax. My meeting with Schaffner isn't for an hour and a half, so I'm in no hurry.

I've got plenty of time...

So, I'm munching on my ham-and-cheese-on-rye sandwich, trawling online when a deep voice from above disturbs the ether.

"Herr Knox, are you ready?"

"Huh?"

"Our meeting. It is two o'clock."

"It is?"

I check my computer screen. Then the wall clock. And finally my phone. Jesus, he's right! Did time just literally fly by? Or did I have another brain fart?

"Yes, Herr Knox. My office. *Mach schnell!*" Schaffner clips in his curt accent. While I stumble to keep pace as we stride towards his office he adds with a twist of a smile, "So, Herr Thomas has disappeared again?"

"Disappeared? He said he might be late. He's picking out a diamond."

"Ah, yes, Amsterdam."

"What? Amsterdam? I don't—"

"No matter. I will deal with him later."

Now I'm really worried. What the hell is going on?

I trail Herr Professor into his pristine, spotless, spartan-like office, trying to tamp down the apprehension rising in my gut. (Or is it the half-eaten lunch I'm about to hurl?) Everyone knows Erich Otto Schaffner's reputation for stomping on lab assistants like so many cockroaches. Tom's survived for over a year; I'm coming up on eight months. The person I replaced—a Lolly Jones—just stopped coming to work; she completely dropped off the face of the earth. Or so Tom said when he interviewed me for her position, claiming with glee, "Schaffner must have scared her shitless."

So now *I'm* facing the firing squad . . .

"Tell me, Herr Knox," says Schaffner, settling into his straight-backed chair behind his exquisite oak desk with his back to the massive window overlooking the quad, "do you like your job?"

"Wel-l-l," I stammer, facing the window, squinting from the glare.

"Please, sit. Good. Now, your work. Do you like?"

"It's okay. Maybe a bit boring. But it can be interesting," I correct with haste, eager not to rock the boat.

"Interesting? How so?" With his tight smile, long face, and cold gray eyes, Schaffner reminds me of Otto Preminger, the Austrian-born director and sometime actor. Particularly when Preminger played the Nazi POW camp commandant Oberst von Scherbach in the movie *Stalag 17*. Both professor and Preminger are very physically imposing and always impeccably groomed, each dressed in his own uniform. Except Schaffner's consists of a dark three-piece suit, white shirt, and bow tie.

For some reason, my dad loved that movie. I recall him, in one of his more lucid moments when he was around, waking me up in the middle of the night to watch it with him. I must have been ten, maybe eleven, years before he completely and utterly vanished.

"How so?" I repeat, a nervous parrot. Anxious to please my master and not sound like a complete idiot, I play it safe. Say what's expected. "Well, you know, Zeilinger and his research on quantum entanglement. Of course, you know. You worked for Zeilinger at the University of Vienna."

"Go on. Tell me about quantum entanglement."

Although not a physics major, I took a mid-semester course called Quantum Mechanics and Reality and attended several coffee talks on QM, which is where I met Tom, who told me about the QM Lab vacancy. So, I dig deep, try to remember all I can about QM and continue about quantum entanglement, the heart of Zeilinger's work. "Well, like you know, it's a subbranch of quantum mechanics. From what I've read, Zeilinger seemed obsessed with proving teleportation via quantum entanglement using entangled photons. You know, what people call *Star Trek* stuff. Except, well, Zeilinger theorized each time somebody—or something—transported, they would lose more and more of their essence, their matter, until . . . well . . . I guess they'd just eventually disappear. But, hey, in our QM Lab here, it's mostly mainstream conventional stuff. But I'm not complaining. I like working here. Really. Really I do."

Schaffner stares. Gives me that thin-lipped, Nazi sneer. I'm fully prepared to be blasted into oblivion. At the very least to lose my job. *What a blithering idiot I am . . .*

"Bravo, Herr Knox," he exclaims, nodding his snowy white head in approbation despite my babble-speak. "It is good you know the work of Herr Professor Zeilinger. A shame he never won the Nobel, yes?"

"But he did get the Isaac Newton Medal from the Brits."

Again, Schaffner nods. Though I detect a glint of approval in his eyes, I'm not off the hook quite yet. He opens a manila file folder sitting atop his desk, and I brace myself for the real interrogation: detailed questions about my data checking and number crunching. But what happens next is totally unexpected. Basically, a bomb explodes in the middle of the room.

"So, I see your father was declared dead your junior year. Is that why you withdrew from university? *Eine Kurzzeitstation?*"

"Huh?" I'm floored, but I have to play along.

"Your father disappeared and your mother had him declared dead. Yes?"

What can I say? It's the truth. So I nod. However, I'm extremely reluctant to discuss the mini-meltdown I experienced my junior year. Due to stress, the doctors said. Like my mom dying of cancer. My dad being declared dead so as to ease the legal pathway for me to inherit their property. My failing grades as a computer science major. All these factors contributed to a brief (very brief!) hospitalization. But I bounced back. Or at least I think I did.

"And your mother, Patricia? She is dead? Cancer, yes?"

What is this? The Inquisition? I stare in disgust into Schaffner's cold gray shark-like eyes and concede, "Yes, my mother died... brain tumor."

"A shame." Schaffner nods. "I see from this photograph I found in your file that she had blonde hair, blue eyes. Very Aryan, yes? A pity, Herr Knox, you resemble your father with your ordinary brown hair and common brown eyes."

"You knew my father?"

"Yes, I knew your father, Richard. Quite well, in fact. When he was a student at MIT. He was my lab assistant. Did you know that?"

I frown. My father studied computational linguistics. Not physics. What the—?

"And so, Herr Knox, with the ordinary brown hair and common brown eyes, do you also wish to become extraordinary? Like your father?"

I remain silent. Transfixed by his cool steely gaze. Like a hawk, Schaffner keeps staring at my university ID as if it's a noose wrapped around my fragile neck. Finally, I blink.

The Nazi commandant shoots me an ear-to-ear grin. "Now, Herr Knox," Schaffner orders, "bring me the backpack. The one you are hiding beneath your desk. Yes, that one. From your sojourn in Paris this morning."

Now the other shoe has dropped.

༄

I'm back home now. Safe inside my apartment, surrounded by my flat-screen TV, Xbox, Blu-ray, cable/DVR, deluxe fridge, computer, and my ginger-striped cat Schrödinger. I plop on the sofa and Schrödinger jumps onto my lap, purring and headbutting me like crazy. So much is happening. So much crazy shit. I can't think straight.

"Hey, buddy. How's it going, Schrödie?"

Lucky for me, my cat just keeps on purring. If I were really crazy, Schrödie would have stood up on his hind legs and lectured me like some scene straight out of Kafka or Gogol. But I'm not the crazy one here—Herr Professor Erich Otto Schaffner is. So is his preposterous proposition.

Yet I realize that Schaffner's work is based on reality. Work funded by a government grant from the National Science Foundation. Or so Schaffner professes.

"You know what, Schrödie? I need to verify some of this stuff for myself."

I carry Schrödie to my desk and log onto my computer. As my fingers fly across the keyboard, my furry friend keeps an eye on me, protectively perched by my shoulder. Searching for the grant info doesn't take very long.

Like Schaffner told me, he indeed has a NASA grant, entitled "Solving Space Science Problems Regarding Martian Modes of Transport Using Quantum Mechanics." Then I check the NSF site, where Schaffner and a Henri-Louis LeClerc from the Institut Laue-Langevin in Grenoble, France, are listed as co-awardees on a QM project. The title of said project? "Application of Quantum Mechanics in the Macroscopic Classical World: Use of the GHZ Theorem and Multi-Particle Entanglement in the Space-Time Continuum Demonstrating the Dynamics of Causality, Locality, and Relativity of Objects in Motion."

From my one physics class and those departmental lectures, I recall that GHZ stands for Greenberger-Horne-Zeilinger and concerns quantum physics and multi-particle entanglement. And Anton Zeilinger completed his first experiments on QM at ILL, confirming the reality of coherent spin superposition of matter waves.

Basically, Schaffner and his colleague LeClerc are getting money to study quantum teleportation. Maybe Schaffner isn't so crazy, after all?

I must have made a weird noise, because Schrödie mews and paws my head. I stroke his side and he whaps me again.

"It's okay, buddy. Not to worry. I'm not going anywhere; not yet, at least. Let's see what we find on the MRO site."

According to Schaffner, the Mars Reconnaissance Orbiter is still operational, taking pictures of the Red Planet, even though the Mars Rovers—Spirit, Opportunity, Curiosity—are no longer functioning. However, when I access the site, the only archived photos are from years ago. Nowhere is the stuff Schaffner showed me: photo after photo showing piles and piles of equipment on the Martian surface. Stockpiled building materials, electrical generators, and other crap just waiting for someone. Stuff Schaffner and his team secretly transported using quantum teleportation.

Could his photos be doctored? What about his team?

"Oh, yeah, let's check out this Henri-Louis LeClerc, Schrödie. The dude who works for ILL. Let's see if they've got his bio and his pics."

And there he is. Older. Paler. Grayer. A ghost of himself. My father . . . Richard Jonathan Knox. Dick Knox to his few friends.

He's actually smiling. And he has his arm wrapped around his wife. Or at least that's what the caption claims *en français*. Plus, his fresh-faced pretty red-haired wife is holding a distinctive black backpack edged in neon-yellow tape. Laura LeClerc, the caption reads.

I'm numb. Stunned, actually. My father's still alive.

And so is Laura—nickname Lolly—Jones. The same Lolly Jones, former QM lab assistant I replaced who worked for Schaffner. Obviously she still does. As does my father, now known by another name with a different identity. Even though I've never met Lolly Jones, I know it's her because I kept her university ID, the one I found in the backpack from this morning.

The backpack confiscated by Schaffner.

The guy who claims he's eliminated the danger in teleportation and you can no longer lose your photons, so that, in essence, you cannot lose *your* essence; you can no longer just disappear.

The same guy who wants me to become his lab rat.

The same—insane?—guy who wants me to teleport to Mars.

"It is no longer an abstract theory, Herr Knox," Schaffner had gloated. "It has become an accepted conventional practical reality: quantum state teleportation posited by Anton Zeilinger and perfected by me, Erich Otto von Schaffner. Yes, von Schaffner. And you shall become a legend. A hero. Übermensch. So think on it, consider it, if you will."

I look at Schrödinger and say, "So, *consider it,* he says. What should I do? Hey, boy. What do you think?"

My cat gives me a dirty look and jumps down. Soon I hear him scrit-scritching away in his litter box. Well, at least I know his answer. Scheisse.

So I decline Schaffner's offer to teleport to Mars. Too risky. I'm too much a creature of habit. A conformist. Comfortable in my own habitat. How could I have known Zeilinger was going to win the Nobel Prize in 2022? That quantum entanglement, teleportation, would finally be accepted. Yet you never hear anything in the news, or from NASA, about teleporting to Mars, do you?

But I did quit working for that fascist. Finally got my degree. In psychology and counseling. I'm now teaching high school students to be conformists. Who cares what Emerson said? I'm satisfied. And that's all that counts.

My life is rich enough as is.

Even the Latest Telescope Can't Tell Us

By Linda Whittenberg

Why does the white-spotted pufferfish
create a work of art on the ocean floor?
If it is a mating ritual, as they say,
then why do other fish get by
with so little?

Why? we ask, as we go about
our own uniquely human maneuvers,
two forward, one back, round
and round the floor, why are we
compelled to do this dance?

This much I know—
no two of us will answer the same.
We're like the tiny ocean artist in this way.
Out of the particular bundle of instincts
and talents we've been given, we sculpt
an answer with our living.

Out the kitchen window—
I see my neighbor
with her three granddaughters,
From a glance they are
a blur of golden tresses. I watch
intently as they grow closer,
skipping and prancing on the grass,

their princess movements
proclaiming all they are—beautiful,
smart, happy, all three in one stroke
of a brush as I'm standing at the kitchen
sink, my soul almost mouthing

an answer—Why? because, because
there is too much beauty to contain,
because lightning can burn and oceans
can drown. We are too much of it,
to know. Too much in it, surrounded
by the answer.

Adam's Apple

By Sam Shada

How much we must ask, "Has our World really changed?"
as I browse through my emails in between online games.
The Machine's got my mind, as I'm talking to It,
I'm texting and typing, and watching Netflix.

The Apps know my motions, so my Fitbit reports.
My Google, My Mapquest, My NFL Sports.
Wunderground Weather & Lightning Strikes Tracker,
My iTunes, My Facebook, My fear of "the Hacker."

In 10 years or so We have changed what We do,
'cause the phone in your hand has coupled with You.
Someone they call Siri, she knows just what you think,
Her friend is Alexa who lives by the sink.

Your YouTube and Your Walmart, Your Bank and Library.
Blue Cross and Aflac, your e-ticket for a train, plane, or ferry.
Big Brother and Visa; they know about you,
Your shopping and browsing, the bad things you view.

A New Age is upon us, some call it a pox.
E-Questions are Chat answered from Pandora's box.
Connected & recorded as never ever before.
Every thought, word, and deed. "We're all really a bore."

Our work and our play just Twittered away,
consume our lives and devouring our day.
We're just pushing minutiae, like our forefathers did,
once dirt farmers, then labor, now we're wikipedid's.

The results of this era have yet to be told,
as our thoughts are exploding in an internet mode.
The past was our childhood, now our innocence's gone,
we've bitten the Apple. "Has something gone wrong?"

Pandemic Lover

By Charlotte Suttee

and the click click of our talisman, blind cat's eye,
slipping into the shadow of the laundry basket like

new moon—we frantically google how else to describe
new moon, feeling too old. Somewhere in the future we gag

for the last time, make peace with all the sticky oceans,
but for now we just want Hemmingway, opposite

of cosmic eye shadows and monstera stickers on laptops,
hipsters with fortunes of our birthday. The girls in this town

bore us infinitely. Cat's eye rolls in its socket, leaps into the throat
of Atwood's Elaine. Pleasure is hard to come by when

the white middle class woman lives in a police state
run by other white middle class women. So we fuck,

our breath gobstopped as the whiskered ghosts whisper
inside our ear pleasures saved from books we've read.

A Sonnet for the Pandemic of 2020

By Belle Schmidt

What does a global pandemic mean?
A virus which rapidly brings death
and hasn't been seen since 1918.
Corona robs the elderly of breath.
To stop the virus we must wear a mask
while labs hurry to produce a vaccine.
Skeptics say it's an impossible task,
many people don't like to quarantine.
Dr. Fauci tells us this could end
with testing, vaccines, and boosters too
and other measures he would recommend.
But some said, no, which they came to rue.
Now we must carry a covid card
to show or entrance is barred.

The Touch

By Mary Kay Knief

Back turned to enforcer,
he extends one finger
across the table
                    to me
and I—cautious—
extend one of mine.
A Michelangelo moment—
                    a stolen touch.
He, now living with
paid caregivers.
I, living alone
for the first time in
                    thirty years.
An outdoor visit.
February cold,
no sunshine.
And "No touch"
proclaims
the watchful person.
                    Tears form.
A month ago,
an indoor visit.
My Love said, "I want
a kiss. Please
take off your mask."
                    I deferred to him.
Ignored the rules.

Now we sit here.
                    Cold.
He's not sure
what he *can* do.
"Just talk—about
anything you want to,"
says the stickler.

Husband, always a
talker—on the radio,
in person—memories
gone. Now, at a
                    loss.
I, the listener,
also silent.

Gloveless hands too
cold. He wants to
go in.
                  Weeping, I let him go.

Hand-Written Letters

By Sandra McGarry

It is normal these days to use technology
to write to someone, to express emotions,
to define a position, to check-in, to explain
a point of view, to offer condolences.

What is rare is to receive a hand-written letter.
The technology available? A pen.
It too is a tool used to commit thoughts to paper.
~
The pen has no need for a computer.
No need for internet connections.
No need for an app.
~
To grip that pen and write can be an act of salvation.
An act of mercy. An act of faithfulness.
An act of remembering. An act of filling in loneliness.
An act of forgiveness for past transgressions. An act
of passing on who we are and where we've been.
An act of protest. An act of discovery. An act of pain.
An act of remorse. An act of alleluia. An act of gratitude
for having lived so long and still learned so little.
An act of rebellion. 56 signers who pledged their lives,
fortunes, and sacred honor. An act of self-caring.
An act of love that centers the heart of things.
~
The stamp is crooked and upside down.
The print is free-range over the envelope's front.
The addressee reads: **To Grams.**
The letter's contents, a child's view of the world—
It is filled with I's dotted with little circles.

This letter a prized possession.
A reminder of delight ... receiving the exceptional.

Median

By Michael Pickard

My hands shook as I sorted through the mail delivered by our robotic postman. Two envelopes in, I found a registered letter to our daughter Sarah, in care of me and my husband Robert. It was identical to the one our son, William, had received four years earlier, except for the recipient's name. Sarah's tenth birthday was coming up, and the federal government never forgot how children were mandated to celebrate. Because I knew what the beige envelope contained, I hid it under the ceramic elephant on the foyer table. I wanted Rob home when we opened it, even though his reaction was predictable.

After school, Sarah acted as William's tutor, helping him with algebra. She was patient, letting her high school freshman brother discover answers for himself. As a former schoolteacher, I was astounded with her intelligence and empathy, which made the receipt of her letter even more painful.

Rob got home on time, and we exchanged our standard hug and polite kiss. While the spaghetti noodles boiled and the meat sauce simmered, I led Rob to the entry and slid Sarah's letter out from under the elephant.

He snatched it from me and waved it. "Finally."

The letter was no cause for celebration. "What do you mean, finally?"

"I was worried they'd leave Sarah out. Weren't you?"

Rob and I often had differences of opinion, especially regarding Sarah. "You know very well what the result will be. The procedure will cripple her spark, her intelligence, how intuitive she is—"

"All things that bug the crap out of me. You've seen how she acts, like she's better than us. If she's going to survive in the world, she needs to be more normal."

At Sarah's last parent-teacher conference, Ms. Juris had made a similar comment. Sarah often disrupted the class by asking "difficult questions that extended past classroom material." It didn't matter that she'd gotten straight As since kindergarten.

"Well, after she's dumbed down, you won't be *bugged* anymore."

I stormed out of the foyer to tend to dinner.

Decades ago, a brutal debate had raged in Congress about how to address the exponential growth in gun violence. The resulting ill-conceived compromise became known as the Normalization of Behavior Act. In exchange for keeping the Second Amendment intact, an experimental technology to "adjust individuals' irrational beliefs about the effectiveness of violence" was passed and signed into law.

Citizens' DNA and their brains were modified to eliminate those tendencies. And to make it fair, no matter their race or economic status, the procedure was performed on everyone. It took years, but eventually gun violence dropped to nearly zero after the bulk of the population had visited the Adjustment Centers. I'd invoked the Canadian part of my dual citizenship and avoided the procedure when we moved to Chicago.

The law also required every child to have the procedure on their tenth birthday. William was already a member of its third generation because Robert took him to the Adjustment Center without mentioning it to me.

It was Sarah's turn, and my heart broke. "Rob, she's brilliant. You've seen what she's capable of. How many artificial intelligence apps has she created?"

"Who keeps track? She'll still be able to program. It's not like she's getting a lobotomy, for cripes sake."

"No, the procedure will just suck the spirit out of her."

After we immigrated and I refused to be adjusted, I went to the library and copied the technical terms from the government's original announcement into my phone. In small print, the procedure focused on the amygdala, striatum, and ventromedial hypothalamus of the brain—whatever they are.

One of the unfortunate side effects of the "adjustment" was that everyone's intelligence, zest for life, and enthusiasm all "evened out," to quote the government press release issued a year after the adjustments began. Protests had made no difference. Petitions for reversal fell on deaf ears. Lawsuits didn't do any good. Hundreds of them had failed, all the way up to the Supreme Court, whose members had agreed to undergo the procedure only under pressure from groups on both sides of the aisle, who called the justices hypocrites for avoiding it.

Our current president, who'd undergone the procedure as a child, ran on a platform to require anyone who'd avoided the procedure to be adjusted. That included research scientists responsible for the ongoing maintenance of the procedure handed down by their predecessors.

Because I didn't take Sarah on the scheduled date and time, a Health and Human Services employee named Ms. Wiggins visited us. "I'm here to personally escort Sarah to the Adjustment Center."

"No thank you. I'll take her when I'm ready." Which would be never. The intruder was too large and too strong and bullied her way past me. Sarah came into the foyer, probably from hearing the commotion.

"You must be Sarah." Wiggins reached out.

I shoved her arm away. "I said, you have to leave. Now."

The more she fought, the harder I fought back. Only when streaks of blood appeared on Wiggins' arm did I realize I'd clawed her to prevent the bureaucrat from taking my baby.

Worse for wear and bleeding, Wiggins called the police. When they arrived, she told the story from her perspective. I was handcuffed, taken to the local police station, and booked for assault and disorderly conduct.

I heard their chatter from the back seat. "See, that's what happens when somebody skips their adjustment."

Rob bailed me out but chastised me all the way home about my dereliction of duty. I had to return to court to plead. Rob called an attorney friend, but I refused to use him as my counsel.

The next day, with Rob in the gallery but the children at school, I was called before the judge. At his age, he surely had been adjusted. Still, I hoped he'd listen to reason.

"Your Honor, I plead guilty. However, I believe my actions were justified."

Rob, sitting behind me, coughed.

"Really? The HHS worker who visited your home suffered a trauma that will put her on disability for months."

What kind of argument would resonate with the judge? Something personal perhaps. "If someone came for your child or grandchild who showed amazing potential, how would you react? It's not like I don't understand the reason for Normalization of Behavior. And I'll even admit that it has achieved its purpose."

"Why then, Ms. Miller, did you object when it was time for your daughter—Sarah, is it?—to undergo the mandatory procedure for all US citizens?"

"Simple. The procedure is unnecessary for Sarah. She's never been violent, and she never will be."

"A weak argument. Your attack on Ms. Wiggins shows violent tendencies run in your family."

My attention was grabbed by the appearance of Sarah being escorted into the courtroom. The bailiff with her had a private chat with the judge.

The judge adjusted his glasses. "It seems your daughter has something to say she claims is relevant to your case." He pointed at my table. "Young lady, please join your mother."

Sarah ran over, threw her arms around me, and buried her face against my body. I stroked her brown hair, muttering, "It'll be okay. You'll be okay."

"Sarah?" asked the judge. "What do you wish to share with the court?"

"My mother was just trying to protect me from harm. Isn't that what parents are supposed to do?" She wiped tears from her eyes, stood erect, and faced the bench. "We just finished a module on statistics in school. My class project was the consequences of the Normalization of Behavior law."

"Really?" The judge cleaned off his classes and put them back on. "And what were your conclusions? That violence is at a historic low?"

"If that was my report's conclusion, my teacher would have given me an F."

I stifled a chuckle. Sarah's unwillingness to settle for good enough was one of the things I loved about her. I gave her hand a squeeze.

Sarah continued, "As a country, America is becoming more isolated. Scientific breakthroughs are occurring... but not here. For example, IBM's patents have increased every year, but they all come from offshore laboratories."

The judge nodded with a pleased grin. "Even a smart young lady like yourself can't argue with the results."

"Not with the results, but with the unintended consequences." Sarah glanced at me. She didn't need my approval to continue making her argument. "For example, did you know Russia, North Korea, and China routinely attack our infrastructure? That provocations of hostility against their neighbors have been on a steady increase since the law's ten-year anniversary? Given the lack of responses by our military, America seems ineffective."

"Is that so?" The judge spoke the words as if in slow motion. Was that concern or skepticism on his face? I couldn't tell.

"It's even worse. America has become a mediocre democracy waiting to be conquered."

"That is quite a claim." The judge stared at the bailiff, as if she could provide counsel. "If true, these findings are well beyond the scope of this hearing, the assault of a government worker by your mother."

Sarah looked at me. "Can I tell him about William?"

The experience had been a disaster, but maybe a personal story would get through to the judge. "Go ahead."

"My brother William came down with an illness. His doctor's AI consultant had no suggestions for treatment. But I couldn't stand by and let my brother die. So I did my own research and found a drug that would treat William's condition. It was available by mail-order from Canada so Mom ordered it. At first, it was like a miracle. But then . . ." Sarah hugged me, her body shaking.

I continued the story. "I notified William's doctor, who seemed astonished at how well the drug worked. But a week later, William's condition was so bad, he was hospitalized. Because the doctor depended on his AI consultant to identify drug interactions, he didn't advise us about one between the drug from Canada and the medications William was already taking. We almost lost him." I held back tears.

"I'm very sorry. It sounds like William's physician was negligent. What does this have to do with Normalization of Behavior?"

Sarah looked over her shoulder at her father. He shook his head. She wiped her eyes and looked straight ahead. "Your Honor, everyone who submits to the procedure loses some of their intellect. Intelligence test results over the last century substantiate my theory." She glanced at me. "I don't think there's anyone smart enough to update the AI assistants. I know because I write AI apps myself. Doctors depend on them so heavily, they're providing out-of-date health care advice. The mortality rate in America has been on the rise. I can show you the numbers."

"That's quite an indictment. Let's pretend that everything you've presented is true. What would you have us do? Repeal the law?"

"Shouldn't it be reevaluated now that we have historical information to evaluate its effects?" I asked.

"My mother is right. Look around the world. No other country has adopted our mind-altering procedure and yet they continue to have low incidents of citizen violence."

My fate was sealed with my confession, but I needed to save my daughter. "Your honor, both of my children have dual citizenship. Canada and the United States. Can I base my objection to the procedure for Sarah on that?"

"That isn't the purpose of this court session, even though the procedure motivated your behavior. Tell me, how old is your son William, and did he undergo the procedure?"

"He's fourteen. My husband accompanied him when he turned ten, but it was without my permission. I would have made a formal complaint at the time had I known."

The judge hung his head, I hoped deep in thought. Finally he faced me and cleared his throat. "On the matter at hand, I rule that Ms. Miller has admitted her guilt and will pay a $5,000 fine and perform no less than one hundred hours of community service. The issue you raised about dual citizenship will require me to research its impact on the law. Therefore, I grant Sarah a postponement from the adjustment procedure."

"That's all?" Sarah jumped up. "Mom, you have to get them to stop this."

I tried to calm my daughter, to accept the tactical win.

"I wasn't finished." The judge cleared his throat. "Sarah, your claims are deadly serious. And you have clearly gathered statistics to support them. I'm going to pass along a transcript of this session, which contains your concerns, to the appropriate agencies who can review them for accuracy."

I hugged Sarah and lifted her off the floor. "See, I told you everything would work out."

The judge tapped his gavel. "Court adjourned." He stood and walked out.

The judge must have been true to his word because we were notified that a panel of judges, scientists, and historians had reviewed Sarah's claims and found them accurate and disturbing. So much so, they wanted to understand her perspective in more detail. Sarah was given a month off from school while she and I traveled to Washington, DC, and lived in a hotel. She attended all-day briefings Monday through Friday with people whose names I didn't recognize. She thrived at the learning opportunity from her working sessions, mostly from reports and findings that predated the adjustment procedure. She'd bubble over every night at dinner about the original research behind the procedure to which she'd been granted access. Fortunately, because the research had been government-funded and the basis for a law, those documents were still available in a historical archive.

"The people I'm working with don't understand the algorithms behind the procedure at all. Don't repeat this, but I don't think they're smart enough," Sarah confided.

On weekends, we enjoyed private tours of monuments, the Capitol, Williamsburg, and Arlington Cemetery. An in-depth tour of the Smithsonian by their chief docent filled two whole weekends. Most of the tour was over my head, as if I was viewing props from old science fiction movies.

At the end of the month, we flew home. I was mentally and physically exhausted. Sarah, on the other hand, was juiced up higher than I'd ever seen. She rattled off ideas that had come to her, all beyond my comprehension. Her teachers complained even more about her curiosity and divergent thought processes. I told them to shut up and do their jobs. I wasn't invited back for subsequent parent-teacher conferences, and Sarah's grades remained all As.

While sorting the mail six months later, I froze. Another letter had been sent by Health and Human Services, but not in the telltale beige envelope. Rob, Sarah, William, and I opened it in the living room. The letter requested Sarah's assistance. The expert panel agreed, thank goodness, that there were issues that needed to be corrected in the adjustment algorithms. They didn't say it in so many words, but the implication was clear: they didn't know how to fix the problems and had been impressed by Sarah's intelligence and her grasp of the original research.

To avoid Sarah's long-term relocation to some other part of the country, they suggested opening a fully equipped laboratory nearby so she could spend half-days at school and the rest of her time working with research specialists. I wasn't surprised at their offer. Adjusted people tended to bend over backwards so as to avoid confrontation. William had become more amenable after his adjustments. Robert as well, except on the topic of Sarah getting hers.

Of course she accepted. She told me her plan was to study the system deeper than on our Washington trip. Then she'd educate the specialists about possible corrections they agreed would not compromise the purpose: eliminating violent tendencies.

The work continued for a year, during which Sarah came home every night and verbally exploded about techniques to alter people's minds and their DNA. She spoke in English, but the terminology was beyond my comprehension. I could only imagine how people who had undergone the adjustment would feel, listening to her. However, from the words I recognized, it seemed that she was being exposed to advanced topics in physiology, psychology, medicine, and machine learning. I smiled and nodded, the only way I could support her efforts. Rob restrained himself, and William ignored his sister.

In the end, the assembled panel issued a report to Congress, and Sarah's recommended changes were approved. As a thank you, Sarah was allowed to implement the changes that would be deployed to the Adjustment Centers. In my heart, I believe that her colleagues wouldn't have been able to if she'd walked away. It took six months for the changes to be made and lab tested. Finding subjects who still had violent tendencies was difficult, but the new procedure proved to be successful. After approval, the new software was scheduled for distribution and installation, one region of the country at a time. When Sarah's work concluded, she admitted she was disappointed. Her modifications reduced but didn't eliminate all of the undesirable side effects.

Meanwhile, Sarah's teachers unanimously agreed that she should graduate middle school early and begin either high school or college after summer vacation, her choice. Sarah chose high school and looked forward to the experience. William hated the idea that his brainiac sister would be at his school. I reminded him that, as a freshman, she wouldn't have his classes or teachers. That took the edge off.

We'd enrolled both children in separate overnight camps, at William's request. On the day we began packing duffel bags, the doorbell rang. It was a different HHS employee, with a police escort. "We've come for Sarah. She's eleven years old and past due."

I stood frozen. The nerve of them. "After everything Sarah did to correct your mistakes, you're *still* going to put her through the procedure?"

"If you have faith in your daughter's work, there's no need for worry, is there?"

Sarah came downstairs. She understood immediately who the visitor was, grabbed her shoulder bag, and squeezed my hand. Whenever I saw that smile, I knew she was cooking up some scheme. She repeated what I'd told her in court. "It'll be okay. I'll be okay."

Later that day, she was dropped back off. She burst through the front door, as energetic as ever. "I can't wait to get to camp. They have a STEM program, and I have a list of games for the campers to create. They'll love it."

William's adjustment had been obvious within an hour after the procedure, one that Rob had escorted him to. He'd come back mild-mannered and docile. He'd never been brilliant, but his nominal spark for learning and any intellectual curiosity had vanished.

I took Sarah by the shoulders. "Did you have the procedure? You seem the same."

"Oh, I sat in the chair with a sensor cap on my head all right." Sarah's mischievous smile returned. "I knew one day they'd insist I go through the process. So, when I installed the changes, I added a special one. When the equipment detected my DNA, the machines behaved as if they were working but didn't make any changes." She held up a laminated **I got adjusted** card with a smiling cartoon bald eagle. "Now, where are my swimsuits?"

Conversations with Sor Juana Ines de la Cruz

By Gia Nold

What is love?
It's not queens & diamonds
She is daring
What is dream?
It's temperature that
can create
love
What is motivation?
It's what you are seeking
What is time?
A mandate
What is beauty?
A treat at times a half a line
What is ashes?
My mind passing too soon
What is poetry?
Restoration
What is body survival?
Demons & monsters some beautiful
What are Gods?
None of these elected lions or Viracocha & storytellers
What is life now?
Nothing to prove, engrave   ask Dante
Will silence help?
It can teach without words

Aftermath

By Valerie A. Szarek

My room
is a room
that stares

A Jacob's ladder
dusty attic
cluttered dreams

If I watch the wear
under my feet
I miss the windows
foggy, breached

I look out front
to a man-hunt
out back
to a bush-whack

And check the locks
on my doors

That may be the story
of my life

From a plastic sheet
over the doorway
to the house I built

To four deadbolts
on two doors into
the house I inhabit

I check them more often
after the shootings
and for good reason

I mostly travel
through ceilings

Where no keys
are needed

No manhunts
or grocery store shootings

I wonder which makes
for the better poem?

I usually choose the locks
and worn carpet

But am happier
when choosing the sky

The Wall

By Leni Checkas

I search through the tufted,
mummified grass, that runs
for miles along the boundaries of two proud countries.

In heat filled with cicada cries,
it's hard to imagine ice freezing
the progress of families seeking
shelter from a war pride started.

    Over ensnared tumbleweeds,
    in the waterless acres, child-
    ren stolen from the only life
    they had left—their parents.

While elected officials argue
in their Congress provided by
the many, wearing sleek suits
and strained, sycophantic smiles.

I search in the dappled desert sun, under the shadows
of clouds and carrion birds
but I can't find that border,

    only the dust we all become.

Refusing Meds, He Calls Obsessively

By Lew Forester

Voice shaky, wind wheezes
into his cellphone as he wanders
the cemetery near his apartment.
So tranquil, the lush coverings
of the dead.

Reliving his pain, he picks
through bones of the past,
would pull me under with him.

He twists his rosary into knots,
says the saints have abandoned him.
Clouds fly over his seclusion
like nuns fleeing a convent.
I tell him, *fear and love can't coexist*.

Ignoring everyone's best advice,
he paces under anxious stars.

If sleep comes, sometimes he dreams
of children playing on a sunny porch.
In morning's fractured light
he wakes to no trace, no chance
of offspring from his aborted marriages.

The building's hallway speaks
in rumors, slamming doors.

He makes a bed no one sees,
dusts pictures of those who couldn't stay
then calls whoever is left to listen,
siphoning hope from their sanity.

Not Clinically Significant

By Tara Szkutnik

What I'd like is to be taken seriously

"You're too young to have all that going on."

For the pain that consumes

"I've never felt a stiffer body and I usually work on 50-year-olds."

From the moment I wake

"You must've been dropped as a baby."

From a supposed night's rest

"The Rheumatology Department doesn't find it necessary to see you."

Through a day of trying my best

"We can try you on an anti-depressant."

To remain sane after 11 years of

"Would you like a referral to Psychiatry?"

Borderline deviations

"The changes aren't enough to be causing your symptoms."

On a range of tests

"You can use a cane if you think it helps."

What I'd like is neither a cane

"Your thyroid was in desirable range."

Nor a guess

"There is no sign of autoimmune disease."

But a definitive answer for	"Your B-12 is low, but I wouldn't worry about that."
Numb upper extremities	"The good news is your MRI was fine."
When it's my lumbar spine	"We have exhausted all avenues."
With the slight bulging disc	"Come back in three weeks if your symptoms don't improve."
What you'd like is an insurance code	"How would you like to pay?"
And preferred method of payment	"Our financial counselor isn't in today."
Per your billing protocol and	"Non-payment after 30 days is subject to referral to an outside collection agency."
Standard procedure	"We can only break it up into two payments."
Regardless of diagnosis,	"Your name has to be on the card being used."
Prognosis and customer satisfaction	"Would you care to take a short survey at the end of this call?"

Canaries

By Mike Kanner

Anne entered the room and slowly removed her cap and apron before plunking on the bed. The worn-out mattress sagged, reinforcing her dismay at the news from her Ladyship.

"Bollocks!" Her friend Carol came in behind her, ripped her cap off and threw it into the corner. "Dismissed without so much as a by-your-leave, just so her Ladyship can close the house and escape to the country." Faking an upper-class accent, Carol repeated what they had been told, "'We must all practice some austerity in these hard times.' Austerity, my arse."

Anne stared at the cap and apron in her hand. What kind of a future did she have now? She'd been in service to her Ladyship ever since her dad had said it was service or marriage to a farmer in their village.

Carol finished her rant and slumped on the bed next to Anne. "What are we going to do?"

"I don't know. I've never done anything besides being in service."

"Me neither." Carol leaned into Anne.

Anne sat there, considering their options. After a few minutes, she patted Carol on the leg. "I've my half day tomorrow. I'll go by the Exchange and see what's available. Meanwhile, we've still got to serve." She stood up, walked over to the washstand, and cleaned her uniform.

~

Carol was already in their room when Anne returned from her half day off. She barely had time to remove her hat before Carol bombarded her with questions. "So? Any joy? Anyone hiring?"

"Give me a moment." Anne took off her hat and coat and hung them on one of the wall pegs.

"Well?"

Anne sat on the bed. "First off, there's nought in service. Lots of houses are closing or cutting back."

"Hotels? Anything there?"

Anne raised an eyebrow at her friend. "No. Now, will you let me talk?"

"Fine." Carol settled on the bed next to Anne.

"The factories are hiring."

"Bloody Hell! The feckin' mills!" Carol blurted out. "I'm not doing that. My sister's there, and she hates it."

"Not mills. Munitions," Anne said.

Carol started. "Munitions? You mean bombs and such."

"They're using them up faster than the government can replace them. With the men leaving for war, the factories are adding extra shifts and need workers."

Carol leaned forward and stared at the floor. "I don't know anything about building bombs."

"Don't matter." Anne rubbed her friend's back. "They've made the tasks simpler. And they'll train us."

Carol kept looking at the floor. "Pay any good?"

"Three to five quid a week, depending. And you get paid for extra hours."

Carol sat straight up. "Three to five quid! And pay for extra hours! That's way better than the three shillings we get here."

"We'd have to pay for room and board." Anne didn't know what that would cost. She had never had to worry about either.

"No matter." The prospect did not bother Carol. She put an arm around Anne. "We could room together and save a packet."

"Are you sure?"

"I'd be down there now if they were open."

"Okay." Anne nodded. "Tomorrow, we give our notice and—"

"Head straight down to the Exchange before they change their minds."

༄

They were hired and told when and where to report.

Arriving at seven in the morning, Anne and Carol found they were part of a large crowd. Anne looked at all the women who had been hired. Many exhibited the tidy appearance expected of domestics. Others were in threadbare coats and worn shoes. All were looking for good-paying work. The few men scattered in the crowd were older workers or clearly injured, so they couldn't serve on the front lines.

Almost as soon as they arrived, a man in a grey-striped suit and overcoat mounted a platform at the factory's entrance. A bowler jammed on his head failed to conceal his bald head. He reached down to grab the megaphone at his feet. "Welcome!"

The crowd settled down.

"Before you can be hired, there are a few final steps."

Moans came from the crowd.

The man waved his hand to quiet the audience. "These are very simple and for your safety."

"Heard that before." the workman next to Anne muttered.

The man on the stand continued. "You all need a physical, and then you'll be asked about your work experience."

Groans came from most of the women.

He waited until they subsided. "I know many of you ladies have not worked or only been in service. But don't worry. We need you and have made changes to ensure you have jobs."

"So, let's get started. Gentlemen, if you will proceed to the right. Ladies, if you will follow Mrs. Brown here, we will start your processing and orientation." A woman in a blue serge dress joined him on the platform.

"Well, here we go." Carol grabbed Anne's arm and pulled her along into a room as big as a ballroom, jam-packed with rows of benches and wall lockers. Nervous chatter from the crowd made it difficult to hear Mrs. Brown, who had climbed onto a bench.

"Ladies!" she shouted. "If you will please quiet down." She waited for silence. "Thank you for stepping up. Whatever your motivation, your efforts to support the war are greatly appreciated. I am the welfare supervisor, so I am responsible for ensuring you are well treated."

"Lovely," Carol whispered. "Another busybody minding our business."

"These lockers are for you to use when you change into your work uniform."

"Uniform!" someone yelled. "I hope it's not another pinafore." The domestics in the crowd laughed.

Even Mrs. Brown broke into a smile. "No. Something far more appropriate to the work you are doing. It consists of a blouse and trousers or coveralls, as appropriate." At the mention of wearing trousers, some of the older women muttered about it being immodest and left. "Because we cannot risk sparks, no jewelry or metal can be worn, and you will be issued wooden shoes." Despite some more whispers, no one left at that. "At the end of your shift, you will be required to shower. Soap, towels, and other amenities will be provided."

"Daily shower," Anne commented. "Darn sight better than a washbasin and once a week in a tub."

"Are there any other questions?" Mrs. Brown paused. "Good! We'll proceed to your physicals and work assignments. Those of you who do not have a place to live, see me at the end of the day." Anne and Carol looked at each other in relief since they had no idea where they were going to stay.

Both were declared healthy and hired. Carol was assigned to filling and packing TNT into artillery shells. Because Anne was a little bigger and stronger, she was picked to be a trolley driver, ferrying shells from the factory floor to the railhead.

After orientation, they sought out Mrs. Brown. "Ma'am?"

"Yes?"

"You said that you'd places to stay?" Anne asked. "You see, Carol and I left service together and don't have a place."

Mrs. Brown took a small black notebook from her coat pocket and flipped through the pages. "Ah! Here's a place not far from here. The landlady said it's a small room with only one bed, but you'd have use of the front room and kitchen."

"We'll take it!" Carol declared. Mrs. Brown was startled at the speed of response.

"You see, Ma'am. We only had one bed between the two of us in our last employ," Anne explained. "We're hoping to save money by rooming together."

"Very frugal and admirable. I hope some of that money goes into war bonds." Mrs. Brown gave them the address and told them to report at six the following day to start work.

❦

Despite long hours and hard work filling and moving artillery shells, Anne and Carol appreciated days and evenings off and money to spend. Dining out and the music hall or moving pictures were regular weekend extravagances. They sometimes met other workers at the factory gates for dinner, even during the week.

Carol was already at the gate talking to another worker when Anne came out.

"What's that?" Anne pointed at the paper in Carol's hand.

"Notice about a meeting," Carol mumbled while reading.

"Not another war rally." Anne didn't have the energy to listen to some toffs preach about supporting the war after a day of hauling shells back and forth. All she wanted was a nice meal and then bed.

"No. National Federation of Women Workers. Flyer says it's not fair that we're paid less for the same work as men."

"Job's the same. Pay should be too," said the other worker.

"The woman handing out the flyers said it's about better conditions too. Those chemicals aren't good for us. I mean, I like the blonde look and all." Carol's hair had gone from dark brown to yellow, and her skin had taken on a jaundiced hue. "But I'd rather it were my choice to bleach it."

Anne glanced at the path leading out of the factory. "So, what are you saying? Because I'm knackered."

"I'd like to hear what they have to say," Carol pleaded.

Anne thought about her life. Service had been a struggle, with every part controlled by her ladyship and senior staff. Working in the factory paid better and had a little more freedom, but she still had to deal with mandatory overtime and harsh conditions.

She sighed. "How far is it?"

"I hoped you'd agree." Carol took Anne's arm in hers. "It's just up the street. We can grab a bite before."

⁓

When they arrived, the meeting hall was filled, so they slid into the back.

The Federation's organizing secretary, Sarah Lawrence, had already started speaking. "The Ministry says there doesn't need to be a change because women have never been paid so well. That there were no complaints." She waited for the crowd, which was loudly commenting, to quiet down. "I say that there are no complaints because women workers have been treated like children: 'Seen, but not heard.'"

"Hello, Sisters." The woman who had handed Carol the flyer greeted them. "Like what you hear? The name's Trudy, by the way."

"I don't disagree," Anne answered. "We should be paid the same."

Trudy looked over at Carol's yellow hair and skin. "Bet you'd like some gear so you're not breathing them chemicals."

Carol nodded.

"We're not asking for much, are we? Just to be paid and treated fair."

"Fair." Anne was still trying to listen to the speaker. Then, giving up on that, she turned to Trudy. "It would be nice to be treated fair for once."

"I knew you'd agree. So, can we count you in?"

The two women nodded.

"That's grand. Just sign up in the back and kick in a few bob so we can pay people to raise a fuss on our behalf."

They walked over to the tables in the back and joined the Federation. They were now trade unionists.

❦

Anne had just delivered another batch of shells to the railhead and connected her trolley to some empty carts when she was flung to the ground. The breath was knocked out of her, and when she inhaled, the air was hot and tasted like metal. Her ears were ringing. All she could hear was the high pitch of a siren and incoherent screams. She felt a warm trickle down her cheeks and on her upper lip. When she touched them and brought her hand around, she could see that she was bleeding. She looked toward the factory and saw smoke rolling out from the doors.

She ran to the entrance but was stopped by a foreman.

"MY FRIEND!" She pointed to the entrance. Though her voice sounded soft and distant to her ears, she could tell she was yelling.

The man yelled back, "YOU CAN'T GO IN THERE. MORE EXPLOSIONS."

"BUT—"

"YOU CAN'T GO!" He pointed to a group of workers. "GO OVER THERE. WE NEED A HEAD COUNT."

Anne turned but instead of joining the group, started her trolley and drove straight for the factory. The foreman tried to stop her, but she continued toward the factory entrance.

Once inside, she shouted. "CAROL!" Was her friend hurt? Worse, was she dead?

"HELP!" A pained cry came from under a pile of timber and empty shells. Anne could see debris shifting and guessed workers were buried underneath. Carol worked farther in, so it probably wasn't her. Still, Anne couldn't leave them, so she stopped and started lifting the debris. The wounded helped each other into the trolley. After they were loaded, Anne drove to where other workers and ambulance crews helped them off. Once the carts were empty, Anne headed back in. She still had hopes of finding her friend alive.

"ANYONE? SURVIVORS?" Anne yelled into the smoke-filled factory as she drove forward. She slowed to a stop several times as injured workers who had been able to free themselves crowded onto the carts behind her.

She spotted Carol trying to shift an empty shell that had fallen on her. Anne stopped her trolley, ran over, and lifted the shell with a little effort. She lifted Carol into her arms.

"KNEW YOU'D NOT LEAVE ME," Carol yelled. They clung to each other as Anne lifted Carol into one of the trolley carts.

Once Carol was set, Anne hugged her again and shouted in her ear. "I SAY WE GET OUT OF HERE." Carol gave her a grin and a thumbs up.

After delivering the second batch of wounded, Anne was grabbed by two male workers and marched to the floor manager—the same man who had spoken to them when they were hired—who was talking to one of the firemen.

The manager opened his mouth to speak, but Anne couldn't understand anything. She pointed to her ears, which were now encrusted with dry blood.

He nodded and leaned in so his mouth was right next to her ear. "Miss Ryan, do you understand me now?" His voice still sounded distant, but understandable.

Anne tried not to feel uncomfortable with how they were now cheek to cheek with their mouths in each other's ears. She nodded.

"You disobeyed orders. You were told not to go back in."

Anne realized that she might be fired for violating procedures. "I was looking for my friend." She made the effort not to yell, even though she could barely hear her own voice.

"I understand, but it was a foolish thing to do."

"Yes, sir." She was sure she would be fired or fined at the least.

"But incredibly brave. The fire captain says you saved many lives. Understand?" He pulled back briefly to see if she comprehended what he had said. Anne nodded. He leaned back in. "You are to be commended."

The burgeoning panic subsided. "Thank you, sir. Can I check on my friend now?"

"Of course, and have yourself looked at as well."

Anne walked over to where Carol was being treated. Her friend's arm and some ribs were broken, but she was otherwise fine. They sat together until Carol was loaded into an ambulance. Anne returned home to their empty apartment.

∽

War necessities meant the factory could not close. Anne was back at work, hauling rubble with her trolley and carts as soon as the fires were contained.

She tried not to think about the women killed or injured during the explosion and fire. Luckily her hearing had slowly returned back to normal. Blood-soaked debris reminded her of what had been lost. The discovery of body parts caused her to run to a corner to vomit.

Within a month, the factory was back in full operation. Anne was finally back to hauling munitions and not wreckage the day she was called to the manager's office. Even though nothing had been said since the day of the accident, she still worried about being fired or reprimanded and fined for violating orders. She tried to brush off the factory dust and straighten her hair before knocking on the manager's door.

"Come in."

Clutching her hat, Anne entered the office and stood before the desk. "You asked to see me, sir."

"Oh, yes, Miss Ryan. Please be seated. Would you like some tea or coffee?"

Things couldn't be too bad if he offered her something to drink. "No, thank you, sir."

"In that case, let's get down to business." He folded his hands on his desk. "As you recall, on the day of the explosion, I said you were to be commended." Anne also remembered him calling her actions foolish. "Well, the Ministry of Munitions agrees. Therefore, I am delighted to inform you that your actions are deemed worthy of special recognition."

"Thank you, sir." She didn't need to worry about being fired after all. Could there be a raise at hand? It would be nice to have a few more pounds to put away.

"Are you familiar with the Albert Medal?"

"Not really, sir."

"It is given by the Crown for saving lives. The Ministry feels that your actions evacuating and saving the lives of over a dozen of your fellow workers earned you the award."

Anne didn't know what to say or think. She assumed it was an important honor.

"It will be awarded by the Lord Mayor and a representative of the Ministry on Thursday during the lunch break so the other workers can attend. Wear your work uniform. The Ministry wants pictures to show how women are doing their part. Any questions?"

Of course she had questions, however, she thought it best not to raise them. "No, sir. Thank you, sir." She got up to leave.

"There's one more thing."

She froze in place. "Yes, sir?"

"We'd like you to represent women workers on the Munition Tribunal."

"Sir?" Anne had heard of the Tribunal but didn't know much about it except they dealt with factory offenses.

The manager waved a hand. "There is always a question of fairness when women are called before it. It's thought you'd add legitimacy to any decision. I assume you'll agree."

"Can I think about it a bit?"

The manager frowned slightly. "Of course. Let my secretary know when you've decided. That is all."

⁂

Carol was finally out of a cast and had returned to light work at the factory. She and Anne were sharing lunch in the canteen a few hours after Anne's meeting with the manager when Trudy and some other women they recognized from the Federation came over.

"Mind?" Trudy pointed to some empty seats.

"Do." Anne and Carol had become active in the Federation, helping to recruit and report on factory conditions.

Trudy and the others settled in their seats. "We hear you're to get a medal."

"So, I've been told." Anne was still trying to grasp all that it meant.

One of the women spoke up. "We all think a lot of what you did. Saved a lot of us." Anne recognized her as one of the women she'd pulled from the wreckage. The burn scar on her neck and face was evidence of her presence that day.

Anne shrugged. "Wasn't doing anything but looking for Carol. Any of you would have done the same."

"Maybe, but it was you that did it," Trudy countered. "More important, you ignored the men to do what was right." Anne just shrugged again. Most of that day was a blur to her. "We also heard you've been asked to be on the Tribunal." Although not on the factory floor, the manager's secretary was a Federation member and must have passed on the meeting details.

Anne exchanged a glance with Carol. "Aye, but I've not decided."

Trudy reached across the table and grabbed Anne's hand. "You have to agree. Right now, the Tribunal is a joke. It's all men, and we women don't get a fair shake. This is what the Federation is working for. Women having a voice. Especially a woman who knows what it's like to work twelve hours a day on the floor." Trudy gave her hand a squeeze. "You were in service before, right?"

"Yes, housemaid."

"Going back?"

Anne thought about life back then. Her hours were longer, her pay less, and her spare time controlled. Working at the factory showed her she didn't need to live that life. But, more importantly, she couldn't take orders from a woman who had sat out the war. "No."

"Right! You've earned your own. Your time's your own when you're not working. You've learned what it's like to have freedom. I know you and Carol believe in the cause. That's why you do more than just pay the dues." Trudy released Anne's hand and sat back. "Listen, we know you're no coward. You risked your life for us other workers. We need someone like you making our case. Defending our cause."

The whistle signaling the end of the break blew. When they were clear of the table, Trudy grabbed Anne's shoulder and faced her. "Give it a think. You'd be a great help. As much as pulling folks out of the fires."

Once Trudy and the others left, Carol, who'd been quiet while Anne and Trudy had talked, spoke up. "Trudy's right. You're the person to do it. No one's going to argue with a hero."

At that evening's meeting, Anne told Trudy that she'd notified the manager she'd serve on the Tribunal.

⁂

The first Tribunal meeting Anne was invited to was in the afternoon, so she came straight up from the factory floor. Entering the wood-paneled conference room, Anne saw the remains of a fancy luncheon being removed. The other members were talking among themselves and smoking cigars. Looking around, Anne saw she was not only the only woman but also the only person in coveralls. She was ignored until an older gentleman, whom she assumed was in charge, called the meeting to order.

"All right, let's begin." He looked at Anne. "You must be our woman worker." He pointed to a chair by the door. "Sit there. That way you can get the tea when we're ready." Anne started to speak up and tell him that she wasn't in service any longer but decided to hold her tongue. Getting kicked out of the meeting for being uppity wouldn't do any good.

The first case was a woman accused of assaulting another worker. She had the yellow complexion and bleached hair typical of the women that mixed TNT for the shells. A persistent cough confirmed it.

"Name, please." the clerk asked. "For the record."

"Mary Merton." Anne couldn't tell if her sniffles and teary eyes were from emotion or her exposure to dangerous chemicals. Given the tremor in her voice, she put it up to emotions. None of the men seemed to take note.

"Now," the man in charge looked at a file in his hands, "This says you struck your foreman and then kicked him. Is that true?"

"Yes, but—"

"We cannot have workers attacking each other. Especially their supervisors. You are lucky you are only being fired and not charged." He handed the file to the clerk.

"No!" the woman exclaimed. "You can't do this. I've children to feed. It's not fair."

"You should have thought of that before you hit the man. You're dismissed."

The woman turned to leave and started to cry. Anne jumped up, stopped the woman from going, and held her so she could cry on Anne's shoulder.

"This is not the place for histrionics." The chairman declared. "The case is done."

Anne looked at him and stepped away from the woman, who had stopped crying. "No, it's not!" Anne announced, causing the other members of the Tribunal to take notice of her. "I'm no lawyer, but this is England, and I think she's the right to say her piece."

"Fine." The chairman folded his hand and looked at her like she was a child.

Ignoring him, Anne turned to the woman still huddled an arm's length away. "Now, Mary, why did you hit the man?"

"I can't." She looked at the men and then at Anne. The fear and pleading in her eyes spoke volumes.

"Perhaps you can tell me." Anne leaned forward so that Mary could speak softly. As the other woman tentatively told her story, Anne nodded. When Mary was done, Anne told her to get herself a cup of tea.

"Well?" The chair asked. "What's her excuse?"

Anne felt she was being accused as well but took a fortifying breath and glared at the chair and the other men, knowing they had no idea what she and others went through. "She was defending herself, the same as most of us women have had to."

"What are you saying? You cannot make blanket accusations. You need to be more specific."

"All right. If you gentlemen want to hear." She pronounced gentlemen like it was a slur. "The man grabbed her coming out of the loo and pulled her jumper down. He was trying to force himself on her. Would you like more details? Or is that specific enough for you?"

The room was quiet while the clerk nervously shuffled papers. The chair finally spoke. "Surely an irregularity."

"No, actually, this kind of thing is quite regular." Anne had been similarly attacked a few months back. Luckily she was stronger than the man at that time had given her credit for. "I could give you more specifics if you'd like."

The chairman licked his lips. "I think we have enough. We'll just make that an admonishment, and she can keep working."

A small flame of fury lit in Anne's soul. "What about the man?" she demanded.

"He has a family to support. Next case." The chairman had the decency to look slightly embarrassed as he looked away from her and focused on the papers in front of him.

Anne saw she had achieved as much as possible and took her seat. However, she was not asked to get the tea when they took a break.

⁘

As the war wound down, the munitions works started to reduce their labor force by dismissing women workers. Male-dominated trade unions, which had fought for equal pay for women, now fought to return those jobs to men. Mass notices of firings accompanied the announcement of the war's end.

"Fired!" Carol brandished the notice in front of Anne, who had just opened her pay packet. "Just like that, and benefits nowhere near what we're earning."

Anne was reading her own notice. "Says here we can apply at the Exchange and get our old jobs." She looked at Carol. "I'm not doing it. Not going back into service and kowtowing to some lady who sat out the war in a posh manor and only had to worry about running out of marmalade."

"So what are we going to do, Anne?"

"I don't know."

Just then, Trudy came by with flyers announcing a Federation meeting about the dismissals. Anne and Carol grabbed a handful and joined her in handing them out.

The meeting that night was louder than usual. Many of the women came straight from the factory. It took a while for the speaker from the Greater London Federation to be heard. "We have been lied to! We have been lied to by politicians we had no hand in electing." The woman was dressed in a plain worn coat, and her yellowish complexion was testimony to her time as a munitions worker. The woman continued. "Well, if they won't hear us at the ballot box, they'll hear us in the street. It is time for us to rise like lionesses and show them what we can do." Anne and Carol both shouted their agreement.

⁓

A week later, Anne, Carol, and the other women assembled behind a banner identifying their factory. All wore their work uniforms and munition badges. Anne also wore her Albert Medal pinned to her uniform and found herself pushed to the middle of the front row holding the banner.

After one of the supervisors shouted, "Forward!" the crowd surged ahead, joining groups from other factories. They ended their march at Parliament and demanded to see Lloyd George, the Munitions Minister. They shouted for him to come out, otherwise they were coming in. A line of police prevented their entry. Just as Anne felt sure a riot was about to break out, a diminutive man in a tweed overcoat and bowler came out from the ministry building to address them, mounting a small platform that had been brought out for that purpose. He began to speak, but Anne couldn't hear a word over the sounds of the unhappy women.

"Ladies!" His attempt to get their attention was ignored until one of the Federation leaders stepped up on the platform and signaled for quiet. An uneasy hush fell.

"Ladies!" He started again.

"I'm no lady! I'm a worker!" cried someone, which got a cheer from the crowd.

The man ignored the remark. "As I was saying, the decision about closing factories and benefits was made by elected officials."

"I didn't vote for 'em!" was the answer to the last.

Before he could start again, several women pressed Anne forward. "Anne, get up there and tell him what we think."

She got up on the platform and cleared her throat. "We, uhm, we feel that—"

"Louder!"

Looking at the crowd, Anne saw the women who, like her, had volunteered for the dangerous job of making munitions. She saw the yellow hair of workers affected by the chemicals and heard the persistent coughs of those who couldn't breathe easily. Memories of the explosion and all the women who couldn't be here came to mind. She remembered how much she had learned to rely on them as friends. And they now asked for her to be their voice.

She took a deep breath and started again. "You asked for us to pitch in, and we did. You asked us to work extra hours, and we did."

"And were well paid." The bureaucrat stated, trying to disrupt her speech.

"But not as well as the men!" Cheers echoed from the crowd. Anne now knew what she had to say. "You had us work with chemicals that made us sick and outcasts because it turned us yellow. You made a joke of it and called us 'canaries.' Yet your boss," she jabbed her finger into the man's chest, "Lloyd George himself, praised us and said the war could not be won without our help."

"You tell him, Sister!" came from several members of the crowd.

"And when we died because of illness or accident—"

The crowd shouted the names of factories where there had been explosions.

Anne was now shouting to be heard by the entire crowd. "And when we died, you sent flowers but paid our families less because we were only women." She pointed to the Albert medal on her chest. "This government gave me this medal for bravery. Your boss wrote a letter praising me. The Lord Mayor said I did what few men could have done." The official was noticeably distressed at being the target of her attack. "But I can't even vote for any of them."

She took a step forward and was now in the man's face. "Well, you can tell all those high and mighties, we're not going back. It's a new world, and women will have a place in it."

Tone of Voice

By Lynette Moyer

It was low, it burbled
like a bass guitar, swelled
like a cello, grew complex
as the cave of a bassoon.
We felt safe, we women,
curled in the comfy
bourbon of that voice.
Our father, our priest
our captain, our anchor,
our president, pilot, men.
Would that we women
had the virtue of voices,
more choices, husky or
dusky or rich, dark
chocolate or coffee,
cabernet, smoke, satin,
beyond the seductive.
The higher the voice,
the lower the status,
though a pedestal
might replace pedals
or chords, or vibrato.
As girls we knew to
speak sparingly, sing
liltingly, pipingly, stay
musical, soft, lyrically
sweet. Flutes, violins.
Think grace notes,
accompaniment, add
harmony lines. Angels
and virgins, the altos.
Add ambition or power,
solo soprano, running
for office, we became
frank, shrill and off-
putting, off-key, angry,
loud, unlikable, sour.
Simply not normal.
The message is simple
about women's voices:
there aren't simple choices.

Misplaced Persons

By Lynette Moyer

It wasn't easy, the idioms, hand gestures,
remembering to heat water for baths.
They remolded me—created new clothes,
taught me how to talk, to dance—took me
sightseeing, hand-in-hand, under the palms.
Burnt coffee scented the mosaics.
Kissing, one kiss per cheek, expected
upon meeting, even meeting strangers.
But hands that groped me on the trolley
as I rode to school, or at the movies—
were these things I should just expect?
Were catcalls friendly that called me names?

Besides, they got it wrong, guessed
wrong nationality, attributions, all wrong.
At first, I had no way to clarify, correct,
even greet them in a language I had never met.

I imagined a silent friendship with the maid,
black, older than me, who harbored in her eyes
a sense of humor in her room off the kitchen,
where she sewed and practiced her religion.
She offered tokens of compassion, perhaps an
ice cream, pity for a girl with such a pale face.
In her face, I found another hearth,
but home remained, for both, another place.

First, I must forget myself...

By Charlotte Suttee

First, I must forget myself

become grain seed for cowbirds
and, eventually, great earthen chunks
colluvium collapsing into brittle
limestone sinks,
down and into

oh, the deep watery vibratos
and air of clearings

Love with Oven Mitts

By Lew Forester

A red moon has landed on them.

Adam slouches in the doorway of drought,
watching ash from wildfires settle on his F-150.

Another brew empty, his blue jeans are stained
from the deer he gutted last fall. He wonders

what forests still stand to hunt in, as Evelyn
sips soda & watches soaps, grazing on drama.

She siphons sympathy from the kids,
lays down the rules for her unconditional love.

In her sullen lethargy, something
is always the matter. Someone let flies in.
A crucifix hangs crooked on the wall.

He's dusted in gunpowder from target practice.
She wields her need like a weapon.

Both scalpel and suture, this is where love
has left them, in dried up wells within, only dying

trees between them and the unyielding sun.

The Grindstone

By Lynette Moyer

When I fell in love with you
did I fall into that gooey swoon,
that spun cocoon of downy joy,
for the real you or for being dazed
with desire for a man a lot like you,
a man I believed existed, like God
or Santa down the chimney, a man
with your eyes, your exact number
of inches off the ground, your long
fingers, wide shoulders, tight hips,
that wry half-smile on parted lips,
a man called into being to cherish
me, like the wedding vow, as I think
I deserve to be lavished, with love,
acceptance, daily acts of passion
and patience, happily ever after?

Did you then present a power-point
of dogged imperfection, curriculum
of doubts and debts, and like the
weatherman, mild disturbances,
more like a system forming than
the serene dawn of golden wisdom,
a man coolly acquainted with the
night, thus concocted of cobwebs
but afraid to voice, to verbalize
intimacy in blunt fact, naked words,
like maybe *I was also*, so we two
had some serious work to do?
Nose to the grindstone, shoulder
to shoulder, side-by-aching-side,
allowing spit and sparks to fly,
grinding all clichés to dust, we
polished something we called
Version 2.2—not to call it love.

Summer of Love: A Memoir

By Jacqueline St. Joan

The week I turned twenty-one, I moved out of my parents' house. My mother stood by the front door, overseeing everything, taking inventory as I hauled out my clothes and papers, my typewriter and bookcase. I was the youngest daughter, her last baby abandoning her, and I knew her eyes would be wet and bloodshot. I dared not look at them—nothing was worse than seeing my mother cry.

I tried to squeeze by with an armload of books. "You know what your father told you," she whispered, almost spitting out the words. "'You live at home with your family until you're married. Or until you're dead.'" Girls living at home until they were passed from father to husband was an outdated Italian Catholic tradition, and we all knew it. My sister Anita had complied with the rule, but Mary had left home single when she was twenty to get med tech training in Denver, two thousand miles from Arlington, Virginia. Years later she told me she'd been very strategic about how she left home, traveling with an Italian girlfriend and emphasizing to our parents how the nuns at the Catholic hospital would be supervising them. My aunt had had an apartment with her brother in the 1930s before she married. Why, Mother herself had left the Ohio farm for Washington, DC, when she was only nineteen. I was tempted to accuse her of hypocrisy, but I held my tongue.

I, too, wanted the freedoms of travel, of movement, of change. While I was living at home, my mother watched every move I made. I wasn't allowed to buy a car or fly in an airplane, even though I worked while I was in college and could pay for these things myself. But now I was twenty-one, undeniably no longer a child. I had a job and a scholarship. We both knew she couldn't stop me now. I could barely support myself, but I was going somewhere. There was no point in flaunting my power or betraying my own feelings of guilt. To my father, my moving out was blatant disobedience. To my mother it was her last daughter leaving home, as both my sisters lived in other states. I was the last to leave home, to leave her—a loss I could feel in my own body. But to me it was something I had to do if I was going to grow up.

I shared a one-bedroom apartment above a beauty shop on Wisconsin Avenue in Georgetown with one of my coworkers for a roommate. My parents' disapproval was so deep they refused to enter my apartment. My grandmother and my aunt came for dinner one time, but if I went somewhere with my parents, my father would pull his Nash Rambler in front of the building and honk the horn. Even then it seemed to me that their reactions were extreme.

One particular morning in that apartment, I awoke to find my roommate had gone to work and left the bedroom window open wide. The window overlooked rooftops behind the building where an abandoned bird nest clung to a chimney. The bedroom felt breezy but warm at the same time, and a delicious scent wafted through the air, something indescribable—not perfume, not something cooking, not some *thing* at all. I don't know if it was the scent or the breeze or the warmth that made that instant come alive but I have never forgotten that ineffable moment. I now think that whatever happens to a flower bud in May was happening to me. I had come of age.

Weeks later, in the fall of 1966, I joined a small group of Catholic students in a protest march on the sidewalk in front of St. Matthew's Cathedral. The previous week, the US Bishops had made a wishy-washy statement about the Vietnam War, supporting a hawkish position—justifying it, more or less, as a "just war." Georgetown's Student Peace Union couldn't leave that alone. At the time I was working in the Information Office of the US Catholic Bishops' Conference where the press release on the bishops' statement had been prepared, so I was aware of the internal debate and outcome of the bishops' meeting. I had not told my boss that when I left work I was going to join the picket line at the cathedral. Or that doing so was an act of conscience on my part. I don't recall now, but I probably walked from Logan Circle after work, skirting nearby office buildings that shaded the sidewalk slab, and the ubiquitous city pigeons.

I arrived at the protest still dressed in my work outfit—a nice dress with low heels, straight light hair pulled back and clipped into a long ponytail. Although I'd been a Georgetown student for several years, I didn't know anybody in the Student Peace Union. I saw a dozen or so students walking in silence, carrying placards that read "No 'Just' War in Vietnam." This was my very first public demonstration, and I was nervous about all the newspaper photographers and the TV camera. Not only might my boss see me on TV, but my parents could too.

A dark-skinned man in a zip-up rust-colored sweater tried to make conversation with me. He was slim, of a medium-build, and fast-talking—

flirting with me from across the circle and teasing the news photographer at the same time. His hair was dark and wiry, cut short in those days before sideburns and beards. His eyes were very dark, very round and deep, like Omar Sharif, I thought. I wondered if he might be Middle Eastern.

He bounced over to my side of the moving circle of demonstrators, giving the TV camera a big smile, a posed, childish shot that a professional would never waste film on.

"Aren't you afraid of him taking your photo?" I asked. "What if your parents see you on TV?"

When he laughed, I noticed how soft his lips looked. "My parents are in New York doing exactly the same kind of thing. They'd be proud to see me on TV." I'd never heard of parents like that. "I'm Pete," he said. "Watch this." Then he started another game with the photographer. Whenever the photographer stepped in closer to take our picture, Pete lifted his protest sign to hide our faces, ruining the shot. Then he baited the photographer again. "No, just kidding. Go ahead, take the shot," he said, but again pulled the same stunt—like Lucy holding the football for poor Charlie Brown.

A few weeks after we met, Pete and I drove down to the White House with a small Christmas tree I brought from my tiny apartment. Our friends from the Peace Union were protesting there in the cold, and we thought the decorations might cheer them up. We leaned the tinseled tree against the wrought iron fence. About twenty of us circled with our thundering chants: *Hey, hey, LBJ! How many kids did you kill today?*

Later a small group drank beer at the Cellar Door hootenanny in Georgetown. Pete strummed and picked a twelve-string guitar, singing softly like a cover artist for Phil Ochs or Peter, Paul, and Mary. He would lay his right ear down, resting on the shapely side of the instrument as if playing to a lonely child, to all the lonely children. I knew right away he had a good heart.

"And this is a Negro spiritual that Odetta made famous," he announced to the audience, and that was when I realized Pete was Black—light-skinned, not dark-skinned. I guess it depends on what skin you're comparing it to, doesn't it? Actually, I learned later Pete was bi-racial—his father was Black from Mississippi and his mother was Jewish, so in a way I was right. He was Middle Eastern too. At the Cellar Door that night he watched his fingers as he strummed the twelve-string: "Sometimes I feel like a motherless child . . . Sometimes I feel like a motherless child . . . Sometimes I feel like a motherless child . . . a long way from home." To this day that song never fails to make me weep.

Pete and I became pretty much inseparable. I loved his soft lips and his solid politics. He always said he fell for my green eyes. I know I fell for his guitar and his voice—and, later, I fell for his parents. Within a year of moving out of my parents' house, I left my own family and joined his.

In Spring 1967, Pete's Ford Falcon was painted black and gold, the colors of Globe Cab Company. That was how Pete was putting himself through the graduate pharmacology program at the medical school. I remember the plastic box of loose change that rattled on the dashboard when his car crossed the streetcar tracks. In May we drove to the Bronx so I could meet his parents, who still lived in the neighborhood where he was raised.

"The Coops" was an apartment complex across from the famous Bronx Zoological Gardens, designed and built as the United Workers Cooperative in the 1920s. The idealistic IWW builders wanted to raise their children with like-minded people in a political hub where organizing for better wages, racial integration, and world peace were a part of life's fabric. In the photos I've seen of the founders, the bare-chested construction workers are wearing trousers and suspenders. The white one sports a worker's cap and grasps tools in his hands. He is shouting to a smiling Black man in overalls carrying a load of wooden boards across his shoulders. The poster could have been socialist realism art from the Soviet Union. But it was not culturally Russian—it was completely American.

Pete and I carried our suitcases past a group of people sitting in folding chairs in the courtyard, sunning themselves and feeding the song birds. "Good to see you, Pete. And who's this?" one plump old woman asked directly, pointing at me in a friendly, suggestive way. Pete laughed but ignored her question. Then he stopped walking and his eyes focused on the upper windows of the brick building. He let out a loud yodel.

"Just letting her know I'm home," he said with a wink in my direction. "Been doing it for years." He took my hand. "Just wait." Soon a smiling woman waved from an open window. We waved back and walked toward the entry. Above the door of the Tudor-style apartment building, I noticed a hammer, a sickle, and a compass—workers' tools—embedded in the concrete. We stepped inside the small entry and I looked around for the elevator. But Pete grabbed the handle of his suitcase and started to climb the open stairs.

"How many floors?" I asked, feeling tired already.

"Five."

"And which floor do they live on?"

"Four."

I was winded by the time I reached the landing between the second and third floors. I put my bag down. Pete was already ahead of me by another flight. I felt discouraged—they had to walk up four flights! Not knowing any better, I decided this must be a tenement. Oh no! His parents lived in a slum.

The woman I came to know as Babe stood at the open apartment door, waiting for us. She flashed her toothy smile and wrapped her arms around both of us. Born Bertha Halperin to Ukrainian Jews who barely escaped the pogroms of 1905, she had been called Babe her entire life. A short and plump but muscular woman, she was conditioned by regular tennis matches and walks in Bronx Park. Her eyes were blue-green marbles, and she used them to pierce straight into me. I liked her right away.

Sol, a dark man with a round belly filling his checkered shirt, ambled into the narrow hall. He, too, was smiling and offered a hug. What delighted me about Sol was his deep baritone voice that thrummed when he spoke. During World War II, Sol had served in the South Pacific where he performed in the USO production of Gershwin's *Porgy and Bess*. Later he told me he was born in Mississippi and raised "in the kitchens of white folks." His mother was a cook who at that time was living in Harlem. Sol had toured with a doo-wop quartet in the 1930s. He and Babe met in a leftist choral group. His baritone, her second soprano—music sustained the politics of their lives. *Lift every voice and sing, till earth and heaven ring.* They had left the Communist Party disenchanted sometime after the 1939 Hitler-Stalin pact that had allowed the Nazis to massacre Poland's Jews with impunity. Babe and Sol remained committed leftists nonetheless, as were most of their friends.

Babe and Sol's home told me how wrong my snap judgments about their building had been. It was not a tenement—not at all, but a four-room apartment, clean and light, in a building overlooking an expansive courtyard rose garden. The place was functional and complete—every door in their apartment carried its own load and the weight of whatever had been strapped to its back—a hanging shoe bag, a linen shelf, a spice rack. The kitchen was spacious. Shiny linoleum floor. Maple table, chairs, sofa, and coffee table. Curtains, place mats, and dishes all in the green, gold, and burgundy colors of autumn. The coffee table held copies of *Sing Out!* and NAACP publications.

The living room was Sol's space. The coffee table held the *National*

Enquirer, books on learning French and Spanish, and books on winning at bridge. A TV console and big recliner completed the room. Pete's room held a three-quarter bed and one long bookcase with Sol's plastic bowling trophies and Pete's baseball trophies, plus framed family snapshots and school photos. I noticed how in the open windows lay folded blankets in cotton covers. Outside I could see stacks of blankets and featherbeds in others' windows, too. Quite a few women had taken advantage of the good weather to air out the bedding. I had never seen such a thing before.

I sat in the open kitchen, wondering what it had been like for Pete growing up there. I imagined him sitting at the end of the maple table on a weekday morning, one leg folded under his body, scooping Wheatena from a bowl with his right hand, his left holding the *New York Post* while rock 'n' roll played on the little transistor radio with the long antenna. I could picture Babe at the sink, fully dressed for work—polyester skirt and blouse, costume jewelry and makeup—washing each bowl by hand, speaking over her shoulder to Pete, asking if he wanted more orange juice. Then Sol rushed in the way fat men do, looking like they're covering a lot of ground. He was wearing slacks and a tan turtleneck shirt with a pendant around his neck: "I have a dream" on one side, a photo of Martin Luther King on the other.

In their home, the stories in the *New York Times* or the *Daily Worker* —the newspaper of the Communist Party—were important and personal. The growing number of soldiers killed, protests rising in the world, the war on poverty, literacy tests as a condition of voting. Pete's family cared about the Vietnamese women who rushed into the fields with their children, frightened by the sounds of US warplanes. They cared whether the old man at the courthouse got a chance to vote once before he died. For me, the longer I knew his parents, the more the point of view of these news accounts changed. Now these stories were about us, not about them out there. Their politics connected the heart and the head and the newspaper and the checkbook and the next phone call and the next trip they planned and the stuff of this material world that went into making a life.

As a child, Pete enjoyed the acceptance and love of a wide circle of his parents' friends, but sometimes their politics caused him anxiety. He told me that before he would invite a school friend to his home, he would rush ahead to hide the *Daily Worker* that might be lying open on the coffee table. For an eight-year old, the fear that a friend would find out that his parents had once been communists might mean they would tell their parents, who would tell someone in the government and his parents might be sent off to jail. Or executed like the Rosenbergs. He had heard the talk around the table and over the phone. His mother's cousin had packed up his boys and wife and gone underground to hide from the FBI. Young Pete wasn't sure exactly what "underground" meant, but he knew he'd not seen his cousins since they left. These stories revealed to me the sinister side of the FBI (where several of my relatives had worked), especially J. Edgar Hoover's efforts to undermine Dr. King and the civil rights movement in the early years.

In 1965 and with his parents' support, Pete had traveled to Louisiana to work with the Congress of Racial Equality in the heart of Ku Klux Klan country. CORE's leader, James Farmer, was devoted to nonviolent direct action but was the ongoing target of violence himself. Pete participated in marches in Bogalusa, where he was put up in a house that was threatened with firebombing. Pete told me that one night he ended up in the front seat of Farmer's decoy car as they drove through the back roads of Louisiana. "Use this if you need to," someone said to him, shoving a revolver onto Pete's lap. He was terrified, and didn't even know how to use a gun. Even worse, along the way, one of the cars ran out of gas and they had to hide in the fields until someone brought them a can of fuel.

Babe worked as a bookkeeper for the local furniture workers union in lower Manhattan, and Sol was a union shop steward and factory line worker at the Bilt-Rite baby carriage company in Brooklyn. Their things might have been inexpensive, faded, or worn, but no matter. What money they had, they spread around to whatever interested them. Pete went to summer camp and took lessons in whatever interested him. I remember Babe writing a five-dollar check and putting it in an envelope addressed to the Southern Christian Leadership Conference. Other envelopes like that one, penned with her careful hand, were often laid out on the telephone bench near the front door, waiting to be taken to the mail slot downstairs. Pete's family sometimes spent weekends in the country, driving up the Hudson Valley and staying with friends. They found ways to enjoy the ocean and play pinochle or bridge with friends. And after Pete and I married, his parents sent us a little money from time to time, even though we never asked for it.

Although I now realize I had been brought up working class—my father a union musician sometimes out of work and my babysitting stay-at-home mother—I had nevertheless thought I was from a middle-class family aspiring to marry into the upper middle class. The quality of possessions was always emphasized over quantity, while at the same time there was never enough money for vacations—unless Daddy also had a job wherever we were going—or for lessons of any kind, including music lessons. We never went to camp or joined anything that wasn't connected to our school or church. I don't remember my parents donating to anything other than the Sunday collection basket as it passed by. With one paycheck and three daughters, my parents gave practical gifts, like clothes. Yet my upbringing had subtly told me to look down on people who didn't want Waterford crystal or Lenox china. So when I met Babe and Sol, I was confused about how they lived, not knowing the nature of beauty or style in a fourth-floor walk-up. But when I curled up under the old blanket with its cotton cover fastened at the corners with safety pins, the cover was warm and soft against my face and cool and clean against my bare skin. I felt comforted in a strange place in a strange city, at the start of a life I had never imagined I would live without my own parents in it.

Pete and I had tried the *Guess Who's Coming to Dinner* route with my parents, but that failed. It was the same year that film won an Academy Award, so I was foolishly hopeful that they would be gracious. I'd invited the two of us to their house without mention of Pete's mixed racial background. Instead of conversation, we spent a silent hour being ignored, eating my mother's meatloaf on TV trays in the living room. No, they were not Spencer Tracy and Katherine Hepburn—although, honestly, now I think they would have liked to have been.

I married Pete and was estranged from my parents for the next fifteen years. Before I met Pete, I had been having difficulty imagining my future. I still had another year to complete my bachelor's degree at Georgetown in international affairs, but my interest in that field was waning. I knew I'd never be able to defend US foreign policy abroad, which had been my vague career goal. My interests were taking me in the direction of art and psychology, and I wanted to transfer to Georgetown's College of Arts and Sciences but at the time women were relegated to the schools of nursing, languages, and foreign service. Unfair, but an injustice I accepted at the time. I was still doing office work for the US Bishops' Conference and attending classes sporadically. My relationship with my parents was in shambles since I'd left home, and dating Pete only worsened it.

Although that uncertainty about the future was not the only reason that I did it, I can see now how marrying Pete was a solution to the dilemma so many women face: What next? I now think I needed accepting parents like his as much as I needed a husband. And of course I realized I was making real my parents' worst fear—that I would marry outside the Church, and to a colored man! Sometimes I wonder if I was just upping the ante in our poker game. I had to wonder if I was making a mistake. Of course, my parents tried to talk me out of it, as did both my sisters ("Just wait a year," they begged) and two priests, but I wanted a new life with this man I loved. I was still desperate to separate from my mother, and moving out of my parents' home hadn't been enough. What I did not consider then was that my separating from her so abruptly—announcing I was getting married in three days—could damage her fragile mental state as well. I'm grateful it only took us fifteen years to repair that breach instead of each of us nursing our wounded souls to the end of our lives.

By June 1967, Pete learned he had been selected for a summer job in California with the Student Health Project, a federal anti-poverty program. That was when he asked me to marry him and go with him and I said yes. I watched him move into action. Pete was the great planner, provider, controller, idea man, with notes on index cards stashed in his pocket. We had to get to California soon. But where to get married? The District, where I lived, had a waiting period for blood testing; Virginia, where Pete lived, prohibited interracial marriage.

The laws of slavery had written that one part Negro blood meant you were the master's property, and Jim Crow titrated blood along similar lines. But one week the law was violence; the next week the law was liberation. And (to paraphrase Dinah Washington) what a difference a week can make. On June 12, 1967, a date now known as Loving Day, the US Supreme Court, in the case of *Loving vs. Virginia*, struck down state anti-miscegenation laws as unconstitutional, starting with the one in Virginia. Aware of the historical moment we occupied, Pete called ahead to let the Arlington courthouse clerk know when we were coming. The person he spoke with was flustered and said that they weren't ready for us. "We've not received the Supreme Court's order back from the Attorney General yet," the clerk said to him. They said we should wait. But we were not waiting for Virginia anymore.

"Well, we're coming," Pete replied. "We'll be there Friday, so I guess we'll have to bring a Washington Post reporter with us." Pete was bluffing, of course, about the reporter. But when we appeared on June 16 at the courthouse, no one blinked an eye. The forms asked about our bloodlines, and in the box marked Race, Pete wrote B for Black and I wrote H for human. The Justice of the Peace, who told us he was also a Baptist minister, seemed excited to perform the ceremony—not because we were the first interracial couple in Virginia's history (I'm not sure if he even noticed that) but because he had composed what was then something new—an ecumenical wedding service between a Christian and a Jew. He was planning to use it the following week and said he'd like to practice his ceremony on us—since Pete was B for Baptist and I was H for Hebrew!

Ours was a short ceremony in chambers with four of our friends and a Justice of the Peace prattling on about Adam and Eve and a babbling brook. We rolled our eyes, suppressed giggles, and got out of there as fast as we could. The next day, we loaded up Pete's taxicab with its new $29.99 Earl Scheib blue paint job. Then Pete and I, like thousands of young people that summer, headed to San Francisco, where we lived in Haight Ashbury. After all, it was the Summer of Love.

Morning in the Penultimate

By Janet Kamnikar

We both awake at 7 a.m.,
no alarm clock needed.
It's good to still be in sync.

I make the coffee, measuring out
water and grounds enough for a big pot.
Should we be drinking this much?

When I empty the dishwasher, I notice
the plates' crazed finish, two with chips.
But getting new ones seems foolish at this point.

The calendar shows a rare week
with only one appointment, and it is just
a routine, stress-free dental check.

We eat muffins, drink coffee,
talk about what our day will hold.
I intend to call my brother,

hoping it's a good day
in his ever-narrowing world,
hoping he still remembers me.

Outside, a glaze of frost softens
the lawn's green to a subtle shade—
not mint, not sage—I have no word for it.

After a long summer, fall
has sneaked up on us: the frost, the golden leaves,
the martyred flowers.

No doubt winter will do the same.

Things to Do While Trying to Fall Asleep

By Lynda La Rocca

Punch the pillow
Watch passing car headlights make patterns on the wall
Wonder what the dog is dreaming
Wonder what it's like to be a dog
Count backwards from five hundred
Think about spiders crawling across the ceiling
Tighten and relax the glutes
Plan what to eat for breakfast
Remember favorite movie lines
(Frankly, my dear, I don't give a damn.
Here's looking at you, kid.
There's no place like home.
I *am* big... It's the pictures that got small.)
Turn over Turn over Turn over
Listen to my husband's breathing
Touch his skin each time he snores

In the Secret Room

By Mary Kay Knief

My tree, my comfort,
green a week ago
now yellow and red.
It feels like summer
but fall surrounds us.

A leafy front-porch room—
my husband sat there
most summer days,
called out to neighbors
walking their dogs.

Last month those passersby
came for a celebration of life
for the man on the porch
behind the tree
with his beloved cat.

In another week
I'll be totally exposed
as though naked
when, really, it will be
the tree that shows itself bare.

Snows will fall
winds will twist the branches.
May they hold tight
for another summer and
a new secret room

where I will sit,
not saying a word
a presence, not the same presence
not even the same person
who once sat with him.

When the Crabapple Blooms

By Linda Whittenberg

First thing I noticed was the cast
on his old dog's leg; then, the owner's face,
drawn with grief. That's when I knew
his wife had passed on. The two of them,
dog and man, wore heavy harnesses of sadness.
I wondered if the German Shepherd's mishap
at the dog park represented a manifestation
of his bereavement. Everyone had known
the end was coming soon.

As we stood under an umbrella of pink
crabapple blossoms, my friend unfolded
the story of how the funeral director had
welcomed the dog in to see the body
before cremation. I remember thinking,
perhaps it's not as cruel a world as we make out.
Just then, Diane, the elderly lady who delivers
papers and wears her hard years upon her face,

arrived on her delivery route, and we three
were all hugs and sympathy. She and I assured
him it was okay that his wife had chosen CPR,
even though she knew it might break
her chest bones. We make much of letting go,
but who wouldn't want to be alive
where sympathy abides like crabapple blossoms
that dress the world in beautiful colors?

In a Previous Life

By Janet Kamnikar

I have it on good authority
(my mother) that my first word
was "cookie." It figures.

She told me I had an imaginary
friend named My Boy Bill,
that we had to leave the theater
in the middle of "Bambi"
because I was terrified,
and that I refused to wear
a navy blue bathrobe
because in the Sears Roebuck catalog,
a little boy was modeling it.

All of these things happened.
I remember none of them.
I think of my brother,
who's lost the stories
of more than 50 years.

I would like to be his
good authority, but telling
him of landmarks in a country
he does not recognize wastes
vital time. We talk instead
of the memories we still share.
To count off the rooms in the schoolhouse
and agree on which grades were in each,
then to triumphantly call out the names
of our teachers, pleases him.

My crucial role is not to reveal,
but to confirm.

We recite the names of our dogs.

My Lancelot

By Megan E. Freeman

It may be the treats
in my pocket, but
I like to pretend
his unwavering attention
his fixated gaze
his willingness to repeatedly
supplicate himself at my feet
(*sit. down. stay.*)
are, in fact, evidence
of love unparalleled.
If I were queen
and he my knight,
the coin of our realm
would have embossed
Fealty † Trust † Devotion
above a face
so dear, so true
serfs and peasants
everywhere would weep.

Notorious

By Sunny Bridge

I always liked the idea of seeming notorious, but it's hard to pull off notoriety when you're addicted to approval. And yet . . . at age twelve . . . I . . . wore a jumpsuit . . . to school. My notorious mom talked me into it. It was something she had made for me, a sort of jumper you'd wear with a blouse or turtleneck under it on top, but the bottom ended in pants instead of the usual skirt, head to toe a mod seventies geometric pattern of bottle green, earthy red, goldenrod. I was terrified I'd be sent home from school. No pants for girls back then, not even when it was twenty degrees during recess, but there were only a few curious looks. It was strangely anticlimactic, as if all the rules had been imagined, a mist that melted away at the first warm beam of sunlight. A couple years later I was the first of my group to wear jeans to my high school, then my tennis warmup jacket with my jeans instead of a normal top. I traded out my tennis dresses for cutoffs and tank tops on those long summer days at the courts. Sounds so tame now, but at the time it was edgy. It was an uneasy tightrope I walked, between fitting in and pulling away, always out a bit further, just barely beyond the boundaries. Wanting to belong. Wanting to shock. My dad had moved out my sophomore year and my mom wasn't around much. Then, I was mostly notorious for having divorced parents. No one else did. You don't have a *real* family, one friend had said. In my hurt I pushed a bit more, dated a couple of older men while still in high school. Feels creepy now, thinking of it, but it got the job done. I was officially notorious. These days I can't even walk two doors down to the mailbox without putting on makeup or waiting for nightfall. Where did that brave girl go?

The Ice Cream Truck: Normal in an Un-Normal World

By Anne Therese Macdonald

This cot is definitely too small, and I've been on it for over eight hours with nothing to look at but a dirty-beige wall and exactly twenty-two steel bars. You'd think with the advances in decorating, interior design, feng shui, a jail cell would resemble something more than the six-by-eight popularized by the Count of Monte Cristo—maybe soothing-colored curtains, a quiet peach wall, a sociologist or two.

So far, I'm in city jail alone. They'll probably throw in a prostitute or drug dealer before the weekend is out. Break me down. Intimidate me. Big deal. A weekend spent chatting up a prostitute would be a piece of cake compared to staring down a fat mortgage, a cookie-cutter house, three feral boys, a hedge-fund hubby, social media, dazed doses of Disney+, and our favorite punching bag: public education.

Hubby remains under lockdown in Japan for the rest of the summer and can't help out. My lawyer, a mom from the soccer team, is on her way back from Vail. Cory, Jacob, and Michael are with my sister. Actually, not too bad a prospect—a weekend with cooked meals at taxpayer expense; a quiet room; a couple of books the warden lent me; no dishes; no laundry; no computer, phone, or television. Let's bang the bars with a tin cup. *Thank you, thank you for my deliverance!*

Why am I in city jail? You would be right to wonder that, my being as normal as the rest of you.

It all began under a cerulean blue Colorado sky, as blue as the beguiling luster of melancholia draping itself over my fragile being. Boys dangled down in the family room, legs over the easy chairs, playing nonstop video games. I wept that Sunday. I wept for the unending car blasts, the rat-a-tat-tat machine gun discharges, the body-shock bomb explosions that came from their three hours of electronic violence. I wept because I'd missed my mother's funeral. I wept because my oldest—Cory, at eleven—got caught selling his Adderall to a second grader. I wept for the fate of mankind, the loss of childhood, the innocence of young women, the independence of cats. I wept because, in the end, we are all alone struggling on a spinning rock in the middle of an uncertain and uncaring universe.

My eyes red with the tears of unappreciated humankind, I tossed the kitchen towel over my shoulder and marched down the four steps to the family room. I told the boys to turn down the blasting. I told them to stop the car crashes. They barely acknowledged me, remaining dangerously oblivious to my pleading, ignorant of the fact that people die and life slips away forever, or that we can be destroyed by one midnight phone call or one tripwire disturbance by a rampaging virus. But, in the end, I am bigger and smarter, and I come from that enduring strain of Irish-American mothers who eat their young. I ripped the controllers from each of their hands and unscrewed the yellow umbilical cord from the back of the television, pulled out its red twin. I picked up the heavy screen, stumbled to the back door, fumbled around Hubby's metallic-teal SUV, his skis, his bike, his preferences. I shoved the television screen, an unrepentant cause of human despair, into the Jeep and tossed the game boxes in. Cory, Jacob, and Michael, howling like small-voiced banshees, followed.

"Man up, boys, and grab your masks. We're heading to Wyoming."

We sped across the Colorado–Wyoming border, bounced and bumped our way through the dusty, dirt-filled frontier roads. Twenty-five miles across the border, southwest of Laramie—the dark, dreary, dry ravine that Hubby and I had hiked those years before, years before the boys, the business travel, the affairs, the virus. Brakes slammed. I whipped around in my seat and lectured, "You boys stay in the Jeep or be left in this border wilderness to find your way back Hansel-and-Gretel-style." A bit harsh, I know, but we had all been tattered and torn for a year and a half. My remaining ammunition? A paltry rhetorical stash.

I pulled the massive television screen from the Jeep, lugged it to a chimney-like rock that overlooked the dark, dreary, dry ravine. "Nooooooo!" Cory, Jacob, and Michael hopped out of the Jeep, ran to the scene, and bawled helplessly. I envisioned kicking the screen over the edge, letting it tumble and crash down the ravine, cords dragging like ugly tails of plague-ridden rats. Hitting the bottom, the screen would become what in reality it was, a useless amalgamation of plastic, glass, microchips, and rare earths: a powerless wedge of discarded hope.

But I stopped, reluctant to carry out the deed. I returned the screen to the cargo space. What could I expect from three wild boys and a world tumbling apart from a voracious virus?

We headed home and turned onto our street, a street that blends into suburban conformity like a garter snake to grass, like spot to dog, like squirrel to birdseed. I cocked my ears. A sound I hadn't heard in two years. A joyful sound, a sweet summer ditty—the hum and buzz of straw-hat nostalgia. Norman Rockwell resurrected. Dancing musicals, girls in colorful pinafores, marching bands. Trips to the library. My mother's green dress the day she walked me to kindergarten. A rum raisin ice cream cone on a hot summer afternoon. My father (long before he left me and Mom), wistfully exclaiming how lovely life would be if each of us owned an ice cream truck, how much kinder and gentler the world would be.

I screeched to a halt, hopped out of the Jeep, waved down the truck, and pounded on the half-door. The boys cheered at the prospect of reward. They masked up and joined me.

"Want some ice cream, lady?"

"Nope. I want to buy your ice cream truck."

"You can't buy an ice cream truck."

"I can if I've got ten thousand big ones in my hot little hand."

"I don't own it, can't sell it."

"Give me the name and address of the owner or you get these boys."

I displayed the three lovelies by their collars. They looked ferocious.

With address in hand, plan in the brain, I spun the Jeep around and drove straight to the center of town, to the old section, where people actually work, hope, plan, struggle, and worry about mortgages, rents, clothing, and their next meal. I instructed the boys to remain in the car. The neighborhood felt dangerous, and I had no idea about the owner of the ice cream truck. "He could take you—Hansel-and-Gretel-style—and throw all of us into an oven."

They held their stomachs and laughed hysterically.

"Stay in the car anyway."

We were beginning to understand each other.

Cracked sidewalk, couch on porch, blaring music, broken screen door. Owner in sweat-stained T-shirt, tight jeans, and tattoos all over his big hairy arms; shaved head, stubble beard and a ring in one ear. Wiping his huge hands on a dirty, oily rag, the guy demanded to know why I disturbed him and his buddies' afternoon card game. He widened the door to display three scraggly-faced, bare-chested Troglodytes.

Cory, Jacob, and Michael joined me on the porch.

"I want to buy your ice cream truck."

"Not for sale, lady." Tattoo let go of the screen door, which dangled dolefully on its side. I mother-lectured him—put down his cards for ten minutes and screw in the friggin' door—then added, "I've got ten thousand cash."

"Fifteen thousand."

"It's a piece of junk, man," eight-year-old Jacob shouted.

"Thirteen thousand."

I covered Jacob's mouth as we haggled, negotiations hesitant and slow. Obviously neither of us could add nor subtract worth shit. If we could, we wouldn't have quibbled over a broken-down ice cream truck in a couch-blighted neighborhood on a summer afternoon during the first opening after an international lockdown.

We settled on $11,500 and the ice cream inventory, which consisted of five purple scoopers, sixteen drumsticks, a monkey bar, twelve ice cream sandwiches, and a letter authorizing me to load up on more.

❦

The next week, I and my now-productive crew of three tootled around the neighborhood in our redesigned, new-age ice cream truck. The tacky Good Humor motif, scraped and scrubbed, had been replaced by a bit of mauve and purple suburban chic. The boys reconfigured the ice cream music from its *ding-a-ling-ling-ling* to the Nitty Gritty Dirt Band. Unlike me and Tattoo, they made change like Einstein on speed. The afternoons became summery, sun-ray-filled days. We became proud, productive members of a good, clean, almost-virus-free society. Hubby might actually return from Japan before summer saw the embers of its days, and I finally landed all four of us in the right place at the right time doing the right thing, in sync with our new universe.

Rules and regulations. Fat city bureaucrats. "Good 'nough for gov'ment" suit . . . I recognized the guy who stood on my front porch, pointing to my very chic ice cream truck. He had coached Michael's kindergarten soccer team. "Got a permit for that thing?"

"Do I need one?"

"You sure as heck do."

"It's in the works."

"In the works?"

"No, wait. It's in my husband's car . . . uh . . . at the airport. He's stuck in Japan's lockdown."

"How about the permit to park a commercial truck on a residential street?"

"That's in his car too. At the airport. He's stuck, lockdown-style, in Japan."

The muttering, stuttering pen-pusher who couldn't play soccer worth beans—let alone coach—pulled his pants above his belly and glanced at his notes. "Let me see, no city permit to sell ice cream. No permit to park the commercial truck on a residential street. No permit to run a business in the suburbs. You owe back taxes on the truck, and you're not following the city and county food service or mobile food truck rules and regs." He chuckled. "You're breaking just about every rule I got, lady." Tapped the pencil tip on his reptilian tongue. "Get the permits or we take the truck." He handed me five citations.

"You mean, pay the obligatory bribes or go to the gulag."

"I mean pay the piper or lose the truck."

I flipped the bird at his back, paid the horrendous bribes, and sent a poison-pen letter to my city council rep.

*

Now, you may think that I'm in city jail because of failed permits, rules, regulations, or third-string bureaucrats. You would be wrong. I'm in city jail because of the undereducated, underemployed, underestimated tattoo guy who sold me the ice cream truck.

The tattooed totem pole took my $11,500 and bought himself an espresso truck—gourmet coffee; short, tall, grande lattes; espresso; cappuccinos; and ear-splitting Frank Sinatra music.

Worst of all, he took my route.

Even I knew the unspoken rules in the ice cream underworld: you don't take another ice cream man's route.

I confronted Tattoo in front of our soccer coach's house. He accused me of disobeying child labor laws and had already reported me to the Federal Labor Commission for employing kids to sell food-like substances. "So, for all practical purposes, you're, like, out of business, lady."

That night, a milky-looking type from the federal portion of our illustrious government showed up on my front step. He handed me another citation, this one for disobeying child labor laws. I added it to the stack, wept for an hour or two, then called my lawyer friend. She and the fed dude worked things out. "Here's the deal," she told me. "Cory, Jacob, and Michael don't make change, don't drive the truck, don't hand out ice cream, don't put up advertising, and don't unionize. Essentially, don't do jack."

Don't do this. Don't do that. Don't do jack. I had worn myself thin not doing what I'm not supposed to do. My mother died alone in a sealed-off hospital room during the worst days of the virus. As she died alone and untouched, I feared that unless I was with her, unless I held her hand and helped her on her last journey, the doors to my own past would close forever. No one would ever again know who I was or who I had become. But . . . I was afraid during lockdown, afraid to travel, afraid to expose my boys, afraid that if I stepped past our threshold, someone would show up at our front door in a hazmat suit citing me for disobeying rules and regs. I was told don't go near her, don't see her, don't do jack. In the end, my father, who still lived in the old neighborhood, arranged a funeral no one could attend and a cremation no one, especially my mother, would have condoned. But then, my father never did get his ice cream truck.

So the day after Fed Dude left, after I paid all the fines and purchased all the permits, I drove the truck alone. The kids listlessly rode their bikes alongside me, stopping here and there to visit friends, watch a little television, play some basketball, kick around street hockey.

On the second corner during our second round, over by the soccer field, one of the mothers pulled me aside. Looking around to make sure we were alone, she spilled the beans that Uncle Mel was overcharging for the dated inventory. She had it on good authority: her cousin's brother-in-law's neighbor ran a post-lockdown ice cream truck down in Denver. I immediately stopped buying from the crook; stocked up on ice cream bars, popsicles, drumsticks at Sam's Club; and hit the streets. Mafia uncle was not happy. When Uncle Mel isn't happy . . .

༄

So I'm tootling along our regular route. Another sentimental summer day made up of a cobalt blue sky and sparkling, uncontaminated streets. Blissfully delighted neighbors greeted me at each corner. The boys rode their bikes next to me—streamers and used masks flying from their handlebars, bells *ring-a-ling-linging* from their bicycles. I'm selling massive amounts of ice cream at good overhead. I'm making money. Cory, Jacob, and Michael restocked the truck, kept inventory, and minded the accounts late at night, alone in the basement. There were no video games in our lives, no cell phone obsessions.

Two blocks from the last street before the elementary school, I spotted Tattoo and his Mafioso uncle.

"You're not an ice cream man!" they shouted. "You're a boringly normal housewife with a broken-down truck."

"Nothing more boringly abnormal and broken down than two Mafioso driving an espresso truck with gourmet ice cream and Frank Sinatra!" I added some final mocking of their tattoos and zipped past.

They shouted their threats: I buy from the big stupid uncle or they take my route. I told them to forget it, revved my motor, turned up Nitty Gritty Dirt Band's "American Dream," waved my Sam's Club card, and zoomed off.

Cory, Jacob, and Michael, their buds, and several neighbors cheered me on, ringing doorbells to get more customers; adding streamers, used-up masks, and bells to their own bikes; sticking thumbs in ears and flapping their fingers at Tattoo and Uncle Mel. We soon had an impromptu seasonable summer bike rally.

The next morning, the tires on my ice cream truck were flat.

Ah-ha! Underground warfare. I knew where Tattoo lived. I knew where Uncle Mel worked. I knew where they parked their Sinatra truck. I called a couple hooligans from a French class I once taught. They agreed to do the dirty work.

That night the French-speaking jail birds flattened the expresso truck.

Next day, I'm flat.

Next day, Tattoo's flat.

Back and forth for three nights—a tire here, a headlight there, a kick in the hood, a rip of the decals.

Hubby called from his fancy lockdown hotel in Japan. "What's up?"

"Nothing. Nothing. Things are great. Just fine. Nice summer days. Good summer nights. Ice cream truck is making money. Kids working hard. Television and violent computer games over and out. When are you free to come back?"

"Did you take out the insurance on the ice cream truck?"

"I took out the insurance. Twenty thousand big ones."

"We need to talk."

"Talk about what?"

"I met someone."

"Met someone?"

"She's been in my bubble for the last three months. We're serious."

Silent for a moment. Twelve years of teamwork flashed through my tired brain. Flash, smash, crash. Reality eventually crystallized from the broken pieces of confusion: the arguments that had grown more entangled, disagreements that had surfaced more quickly, problems that became impossible to resolve, the rampaging virus. "Don't tell the boys. Not yet."

I handed the phone to Michael, the youngest. Jacob and Cory gathered close for their turn while I dashed outside, hopped into my ice cream truck, feverish and frantically reliving the storm and stress, the Sturm und Drang that the pandemic wrought upon us. My world swirled and swayed, tilted to the side, landed in a backward spin for perpetuity.

Tattoo's ear-splitting, nerve-knocking Frank Sinatra music fanned the flames of irritation and despair; the guy just never seemed to go away. Through the rearview mirror I saw him carefully rounding the corner, unsure of his safety on these suburban streets. He sidled past me.

I left the boys with their phone-dad and geared up my truck. Screech. Scratch. I crept behind the culprit, careful not to be noticed.

Tattoo spotted me and sped up.

I hit the gas, flew by him.

He accelerated, tried to get ahead.

I blocked him near the soccer field.

He tailgated, crept behind like an oversized potato bug.

I sped up like the Formula 1 champs I had watched six thousand times on Netflix during isolation.

He sped up, tried to pass.

Tightened grip on steering wheel, taut seat belt enclosing me, I stretched my back for support, extended my foot to the brake, and decelerated as fast as my leg could push.

Fool! He crashed into me like a wrecking ball on a skyscraper. I took the expected impact bravely: swerved around, gathered my wits, and hit the accelerator, crunching him from the other side.

Twenty thousand dollars insurance? Done.

Our ice cream trucks soon took up the entire street, his head to my side.

No car could pass, no child could cross.

I backed up to take another run.

He lurched forward, jerked back, took my hit fearlessly, swung around, and bashed me head-on—front-end to front-end.

We rammed each other again, gasped, gathered strength, and rammed some more. Whamming and banging, panting, sweating until we collapsed over our respective steering wheels. Exhausted. Breathing heavily.

Now, if I had just turned down "Mr. Bojangles" or if Tattoo had just turned down Frank Sinatra, we both might have heard the sirens. As it was, twenty-two soccer kids, five stay-at-home moms, four coaches, and seven golden retrievers witnessed the ramming, banging, and truck boinking. Four police cars flew into sight, slammed on their brakes, jumped out, slipped and slid over melted ice cream, crushed cups, spilled lattes. They pulled their guns, surrounded the ice cream trucks, and with a bullhorn louder than God, screeched above the Nitty Gritty Dirt Band, "Come out with your hands on your heads!"

~

Tattoo sits alone in the men's cell across the hallway. As they barred him up, he hollered his apologies—his wife left him at the end of lockdown, taking their five kids. He lost his job for lack of Zoom experience, and he admitted to unresolved and quite corrosive issues with which he must deal.

Yada, yada, yada. Cry me a river.

I got locked in my own cell—these dirty-beige walls, twenty-two steel bars, and all. Lockdown here. Lockdown there. Who cares? Hubby's not returning from Japan; I get that. My mother expired during the worst of the virus rage; I'm sorry I wasn't with her. But I stopped weeping over all that. Cory, Jacob, and Michael just brought me my favorite coconut almond chocolate chip gelato, compliments of Tattoo's Uncle Mel. The four of us sit on the jail's concrete floor, bars separating mother from innocent childhood, and we eat our ice cream. We reminisce about the fact that we actually, truly, really owned a genuine live ice cream truck. Okay, so it was more Marvel comic than Norman Rockwell, but what the heck. When the whole world takes a shift, you just have to do your bit to shift it back.

Homecoming

By Mary Kay Knief

Was it our small-town upbringing?
One junior high, one high school?
Parents who went to the same schools,

grandparents a bike ride away?
Was it the similar points of reference?
The churches, the grocery stores,

the same good teachers?
How we rode our bikes
across town without helmets

or parental concerns and
ambled home from school
with a crowd of kids?

On vacations to the mountains
we wondered why we lived where
dirt-filled winds made it hard to concentrate,

the awful smell of
cattle crowded together,
being fattened for the best steaks.

We moved out into the world
not knowing what would be next,
but wanting to be good people.

We thought we would not look back.

and another thing they never tell you...

By Megan E. Freeman

and another thing they never tell you

is the complete invisibility
that comes with being
female and middle aged

walking in Denver
along the pedestrian artery
connecting art museum
and bookstore

seen only once
by a dark-haired
tourist child
dawdling behind
her Middle Eastern family

even she has to look three times
before I come into focus

then a few skips forward
and she is back in the circle
of her father's awareness

and I am gone again

Going Under

By Lynda La Rocca

Tonight
I am saying good-bye to my breasts.
At least,
that is,
I'm trying.
Firm and round,
the nipples flushed and pink,
they look so nice,
so normal,
they don't know what waits for them
come morning.

I've never parted with
myself before.
What does a person say?
"Good luck" is out of the question
as is, "Till we meet again."

For days now
I've been counting
every hour
all the minutes
waking in the dark
to red
numbers
glowing
ticking
down my time.

Tomorrow
I'll be living in
a body
flatter
lighter,
heading toward what's called
recovery.

I'll be wondering where I've gone.

Backing Out of the Driveway

By Sandra McGarry

In my neighbor's yard one red rose gives its face to the light.
I stop the car. Roll down the window.

The petals are soft and flat. The stem thorny and strong.
The radiance...

I'm reminded of the great cathedrals. Those stained glass windows.
How the storytelling in them calls on the sun.

Before I drive on, I write this on the slate of my heart.

> This rose
> slows
> everything
> down.
>
> Breaks
> Covid Time
> (the new normal)
> into pieces
>
> imbues a softness,
> a clarity,
> unmasks a truth—

How miracles of light brew in the teapot of life.
They pour daily into the streets and avenues of days.

A vessel is all that's needed to hold them.

The Slow Cloud Days

By David E. Sharp

Some days, all you can do is watch the clouds make shapes as they roll across the sky. That's the situation as I see it. With my back propped against a tree and my legs sprawled across the cartoonishly green grass, I stare at the sky. It's who-cares-o'clock on a Sunday afternoon, the kind of afternoon that almost lets you forget the start of a new school week lurking just one little calendar square away.

Jenna Ludmeyer sits next to me.

"That one looks like a turtle," I say. "You think?"

Jenna shrugs. "I would have said a cumulus."

I shoot her a sideways glance. "That's so literal, Jenna. It defeats the whole purpose of watching clouds. They all look like cumulus, because that's what they are. It's the shapes that matter. Look at that cloud and tell me you don't see a turtle." I gesture with my eyes.

Jenna squints at it. "Fine. But like a dinosaur turtle. With a horn."

I tilt my head and examine it. "Yeah. I see it. See how much better it is when you apply a little imagination?"

She flashes me a wicked smile. "Oh, I have plenty of imagination, Michael. Are you asking for a demonstration? Do you really want me to get creative right now?"

I shift my back against the rough bark of the tree. "Let's just keep it to the clouds for now. What else do you see?"

Jenna scans the sky and points. "That one looks like a train flying off the tracks. It even has a tiny conductor waving his hands, shouting, 'Oh, the humanity! The humanity!'"

"I might have said a snake in need of a chiropractor," I tell her. "But I get it. You're in a sadistic mood right now."

"Gosh, I wonder why." Jenna digs her elbow into my ribs to drive home her point. Then she points at another cloud. "Look! That one looks like a garden snake jumping out of someone's locker. I wonder who she's going to kill when she finds out who did it."

We sit in silence for several minutes. In that time, I see a school bus with wings, a lion that turns into a crocodile, and a leaping sumo wrestler. I savor the images as they slowly twist and change through their meteorological journey. I could watch these clouds all day. Not that I have a choice at the moment. "Look at that one. Can you see a tiny hero with a long flowing cape?"

"Aren't you getting bored yet?" says Jenna.

"Not at all," I say with a smile.

"Liar."

"Why should I be bored?" I breathe a demonstrative sigh of contentment, then say, "Just tell me if you see a tiny hero with a giant cape and it will make my day."

She glances at the sky. "Fine. I see it. Now you answer me. How can you sit around and watch clouds all afternoon without going completely crazy? I think you're being content just to spite me."

I shake my head with pity. "You have to get some perspective, Jenna. Boredom is a blessing. What is an ordinary Sunday afternoon anyway? I'm not sick with the flu. I'm not sitting in some office buried in paperwork. I'm not running for my life from a murderous troupe of cannibal ballerinas. Excitement isn't always an improvement."

Jenna thrusts a finger in my face. "And how long can you go, just sitting here watching clouds? Shall we put it to the test?"

"Jenna, Jenna, Jenna," I say and click my tongue. "Always on the hunt for the next thrill. A slave to your own adrenaline. Consider our tiny hero. Let's call him Captain Cumulus, shall we?"

Jenna crosses her arms and stares me down.

I continue. "Maybe Captain Cumulus has a series of comic book adventures all about his daring exploits and dangerous escapades. We read about them from the safety of our own air-conditioned bedrooms. But how much does Captain Cumulus enjoy taking punches from the nefarious Baron Thirty-Percent-Chance-Of-Rain? Or being thrown into turbulence, or dodging lightning strikes, or—"

"Or finding a grass snake in his locker, Michael?"

"Yes." I nod. "That is also a stressful situation that can ruin a blissful ordinary day. I might add it is the sort of stressful situation you still can't prove was me."

Jenna leans her head in close to mine until our noses almost touch. "But we both know it was, don't we, Michael Flatbush? We both know it was." She pulls away and leans back against the tree.

"Anyway," I say, "Captain Cumulus doesn't enjoy the hell he goes through to keep the world a safer place for you and me. But he does it so that ordinary people can have ordinary days to waste away with cloud-watching, long walks, and harmless pranks involving nonvenomous reptiles."

A low growl sounds in Jenna's throat.

"He does it because he knows that excitement and drama are flashy and fun in the moment, but it's the dull, humdrum, ordinary moments we'll long for in our final moments, as we sit in a derailing train, listening to a panicked conductor shouting, 'Oh the humanity.' The tragic truth for most of us is *that* is the moment we will finally cherish the slow cloud days. The everydays. The days that build a life while you're not looking. Once they are lost to us forever, we'll finally value them for what they were. Why not cherish them while we have them instead, Jenna? Why not cherish them now?"

Jenna huffs. "If you really believed that, you wouldn't interrupt all that beautiful boredom by shoving snakes in people's lockers. Or putting orange paint in their shampoo. Or opening a box of live crickets in their room."

"Fine talk from you," I say. "I might add that they also don't use massive amounts of ricotta cheese to turn people's bedsheets into giant manicotti shells."

Jenna emits a sharp laugh. "It was no less than you deserved then. And this is no less than you deserve now. So, tell me how long you can endure a slow cloud day, Michael?"

I wriggle against the ropes securing me to the tree. They're tight. I won't be going anywhere for a while. That girl knows how to tie a knot. "A while longer yet," I say. "Are you sure you don't want to untie me and call it a draw?"

She shakes her head. "You're not getting out of those ropes until I see you suffer. So, you'd better stop waxing philosophical about clouds and get to the begging and weeping."

I shrug, a gesture made difficult by the ropes, and say, "Then I guess we'll have to see who can watch clouds the longest."

"I guess so," she says.

We settle back and stare into the sky.

Tadasana

By Celia Turner

Snowflake obsidian,
perfect cristobalite flowers
bloomed in rock eons ago
as earth's pressure exploded lava
liquefying rock until once again
a perfect balance is restored.

It's Easy to Be Normal

By M. D. Friedman

for Brent

I can pass for normal if I really try. I put on deodorant, and it seems to help.
Just yesterday, someone asked me for the time, and I said, "1:36,"
even though I always carry a sprig of the herb in my pocket
in case that question comes up. It's easy to be normal.

A husky-voiced phone survey woman asked, "Sex?"
I told her, "Male." Just like that. At the grocery store, though,
I lost it. The bagger inadvertently brushed my hand and said,
"Paper or plastic?" I said, "It's skin. Isn't that normal?"

Most of the time, if I concentrate,
I can ignore all those variant
meanings that come to mind,
and figure out what others want from me.

Isn't that what normal is,
doing what others expect instead of being who I am?
The most important thing is to try to be like everybody else.
My biggest problem, perhaps, is I don't watch television.

In polite conversation, I have found it helps
to nod often, even if nothing makes sense.
I probably shouldn't even talk
about peppers. When the waiter asks,

"Ground pepper?" I say, "Yes, please." Simple enough.
The problem comes when he says, "Just say when."
I usually say nothing. When he gets tired, he walks away.
What I want to say is, "Whenever the grinder is empty."

Lately, I have started to carry
my own bottle of pepper sauce
for places where ketchup is the only
condiment. It makes things easier.

I wonder if anybody really is normal,
if everybody is nodding because nothing makes sense.
I think I could fit in if everyone stopped pretending,
but then people take too much too seriously.

I wonder if anybody really is normal,
if everybody is nodding because nothing makes sense.
I think I could fit in if we all stopped pretending,
but still people take everything so seriously.

I could be normal, if it paid enough, but it's truly overrated.
It's certainly no way to raise children. I guess I should spend more time
worrying about how things look. Also, it would help,
to occasionally be on time, but then there is always

that poem I am working on that won't let me go.
Somehow, I get by. I have a good life, I must say.
There is really no reason to change,
unless, of course, I spill hot sauce on my shirt.

Bios

Editors

Bonnie McKnight founded Lady Knight Editing in 2018 after spending three years as a freelance editor—but she's been correcting people's grammar since she was two (ask about the legendary fog vs. mist debate of '92). One of her proudest editorial moments was accepting the 2020 Colorado Book Award for Best Anthology for *RISE: An Anthology of Change*. She earned her MA in the History of Books from the University of London and is more than happy to gush about ancient Mesopotamian literacy or Christine de Pizan's Medieval manuscripts or Victorian fiction magazines. She enjoys reading, playing computer games, and doing "letters" (Wordle) with her two-year-old. Join her in The Writing Forge, the Writing Heights Podcast where she, her co-host, and a variety of guests hammer out the skills writers need to succeed. www.writingheights.com/writingforge

Lorrie Wolfe is an editor, technical writer and award-winning poet living in northern Colorado. She served as poetry editor for *RISE: An Anthology of Change*, which won the 2020 Colorado Book Award, and for *Chiaroscuro* and *Mountains, Myths, & Memories*. Lorrie was named Poet of the Year at the 2014 Denver Ziggies Poetry Festival. Her chapbook, *Holding: From Shtetl to Santa*, (Green Fuse Press) is available at www.lorriewolfe.com. Her work has appeared in *The Mountain, Earth's Daughters, Pilgrimage, Pooled Ink, Plant-Human Quarterly, Encore*, and more. She maintains an email list of more than three hundred Colorado poets and sends out announcements of poetry events nearly every day. After forty years as a community organizer, she still believes in the power of words to unite and move people—including poets. Her two-word mantra is "Show up."

Sarah Roberts is a technical editor and children's picture book writer who lives in Fort Collins. When she's not trying to figure out a work/writing/life balance, she enjoys baking, reading, being outside, baking, spending time with family and friends, and baking for them.

Poetry Team

Jack Martin has worked as a secondary school teacher for a long time. He has also worked as a groundskeeper, as a construction worker, as a whitewater river guide, and as a stand-up comic. In 1988 he won the funniest person in Northern Colorado contest at the old Fort Collins Comedy Works. In addition, he holds an MFA in Creative Writing from Colorado State University. His poems have appeared in many magazines, including *Ploughshares*, the *Georgia Review*, and the *Colorado Review*.

Kathleen Willard's first publication was in her high school literary magazine, *Beverwyck*, and she has not stopped writing since her poetry debut. Public school teacher and poetry event organizer, Willard's two books *Cirque & Sky* and *This Incendiary Season* are available at www.middlecreekpublishing.com. In 2023, Willard will publish two new books of poetry. *The Next Noise Is Our Hearts*, by Middle Creek Publishing, is a call to combat climate change through innovation and regeneration, and *Electric Grace*, by Lune Press, shares her love of St. Francis of Assisi. Visit www.kathleenwillard.com to find out what inspires her.

Contributors

Sunny Bridge knows her name sounds like an organic farm, and she's okay with that. Sunny has had several poems published in various anthologies in recent years, including *All the Lives We Ever Lived*, *Chiaroscuro: An Anthology of Vice and Virtue*, and *Encore: Prize Poems 2022*. She's currently working on a memoir of her adventurous life with her late husband, a story of chasing dreams and savoring each day. Find more Sunny at MovableAssets.com.

Leni Checkas is a published author of two short stories, "Alone" and "Pray More," and one prize-winning poem, "The Hope of Spring," and she won two Society of Children's Book Writers & Illustrators (SCBWI) Write This! competitions.

Carol A. Fichtelman is a short-story writer and painter whose work has appeared in print and online literary journals, including: *Dream Fantasy International,* the *Wisconsin Review, Teleport Magazine, The Helix,* and *Glass Mountain Review.* Her nonfiction books and articles concentrate on legal issues and are published by W.S. Hein and Wolters Kluwer Law & Business, two legal publishers.

Lew Forester is a social worker who lives in Arvada, Colorado, base for his frequent hikes in the Rocky Mountains. The author of *Dialogues with Light* (Orchard Street Press, 2019), Lew has had poems appear in the *Atlanta Review, Main Street Rag,* the *Blue Mountain Review,* the *Sky Island Journal, Pinyon, Plainsongs, POEM, Slipstream, The MacGuffin,* the *Evening Street Review,* and other journals, magazines, and anthologies.

Megan E. Freeman is a poet and novelist. Her bestselling novel in verse, *ALONE,* won the Colorado Book Award; the Massachusetts, Maine, and Vermont children's book awards; the High Plains Book Award; is an NCTE Notable Verse Novel; and is included on over two dozen "best of" and state reading lists. She is also the author of the poetry chapbook, *Lessons on Sleeping Alone,* published by Liquid Light Press.

M. D. Friedman is an award-winning poet, musician, and digital artist living in Lafayette, Colorado.

Warren Jonsten, a Floridian, attended college in his native state. Drafted during the Vietnam War, he made the military his career and retired to Colorado. He began journaling during his time overseas and writing more formal pieces, poems, short stories, and memoir as part of his daily practice, a diversion from high-stress patriotic duty.

Janet Kamnikar began writing poetry soon after retiring in Fort Collins. She is a wife, mother, and grandmother; a reader, a traveler, and a baseball fan. She holds degrees in English from Jamestown College and the University of Wyoming.

Mike Kanner recently retired as a lecturer in security studies at the University of Colorado, Boulder. Although he's published stories in several genres, he has concentrated on historical fiction set in the World War I period, which lets him use his career in the Army to add realism to his descriptions of warfare. Mike is currently working on a novel version of his story and researching a story based on the Allied intervention in Russia at the end of the War.

After careers involving lots of writing—newspaper reporter, magazine writer, and public relations professional—**Mary Kay Knief** retired and moved to Fort Collins, CO. Because of classes she took through CSU OLLI (Osher Lifelong Learning Institute) and with her B.S. degree in radio-television and her M.S. in mental health mass communications (really), poetry became her new medium. She has had poems published in the *High Desert Journal, Still Crazy, Colorado Life Magazine,* and *Pooled Ink*—the first anthology from Northern Colorado Writers.

Lynda La Rocca is a New York City—born poet and freelance writer who has also worked as a reporter for the *Asbury Park* (NJ) *Press* and a teaching assistant at Colorado Mountain College in Leadville, Colorado. Her four poetry chapbooks include *The Stillness Between* (2009, Pudding House Publications), *Spiral* (2012, Liquid Light Press), and *Unbroken* (2023, Kelsay Books); her individual poems have appeared in such publications as *The New York Quarterly; Frogpond* (Haiku Society of America); *THINK: A Journal of Poetry, Fiction, and Essays; The Colorado Sun*; and *Encore* (National Federation of State Poetry Societies, Inc.). La Rocca was the 2020 winner in the poetry category of the Soul-Making Keats Literary Competition, a National League of American Pen Women arts-outreach program, and a "Top-Four" winner in the 2021 Maria W. Faust Sonnet Contest. She lives in Salida, Colorado, with her writer-photographer husband Steve Voynick.

Katie Lewis lives in the shadow of the Rocky Mountains with their partner, their furry son, and a vast collection of geekdom sundries. When not at their computer, they can be found rolling multi-sided dice to save the world.

Anne Therese Macdonald's short stories have appeared in *Best American Mystery Stories* (2019), *Dublin Quarterly: International Literary Review, Blue Earth Review, Matter Journal*, and other American and Irish anthologies and journals. A novel, *A Short Time in Luxembourg*, was published in 2004. www.annetheresemacdonald.com.

Sandra McGarry lives in Fort Collins. A former elementary school educator for twenty-eight years. Retired. Enjoys the discipline of sitting in the chair until the words appear . . . Laughs a lot. Published poet. Loves the ocean. Finds money. Grateful for friendships.

Lynette Moyer returned to her native Colorado after living most of her adult life in other locations, including Brazil, Kentucky, Wisconsin, and Virginia. She taught English literature, humanities, and many composition courses at Virginia Tech while also raising three daughters. She has published short fiction, poetry, and is currently working on a series of mystery novels. She published a poetry collection, *Catch & Release*, in 2023.

Gia Nold is the author of three chapbooks of poetry. Gia holds a Master of Fine Arts from Naropa University. Her latest works have appeared in *63 Channels, Blazing Stadium*, and *MadBlood*, among others. Gia is a native of Lima, Perú, who lives in Evergreen, CO.

Michael Pickard's writing blends elements from his professional work in technology with his unbounded imagination. His catalog of work includes nine science fiction novels and two children's books. Dozens of his juried short stories have been published, including "Hardwired," which won a Ray Bradbury Creative Writing Prize in 2005. Universes and societies in Pickard's immersive prose entertain and inform readers, who engage with themes embedded in his stories. The first installment of his three-volume detective epic, *Creative Deductions*, was recently published.

Emily Rodgers-Ramos is the author of *Riding the Double Helix*. Her poetry has appeared in the *Dry Creek Review*, the *Greyrock Review, Nanny Fanny,* the *Lilliput Review, the Progenitor Art and Literary Journal: Speak Peace,* and *Chiaroscuro: An Anthology of Virtue and Vice.*

Belle Schmidt is a Canadian-born poet and essayist who has published four chapbooks and three book-length poetry collections. Her work has appeared in numerous anthologies and magazines both in the U.S. and internationally. She lives in Fort Collins with husband Hans-Peter.

Sam Shada is a philosopher/poet sharing verses that stimulate thought.

David E. Sharp is a noisy librarian. His *Lost on a Page* books tell the story of fictional characters, awakened to their true nature, who seek deadly vengeance upon their authors. Had this been an autobiographical work, David might not be with us today.

Jacqueline St. Joan writes fiction, nonfiction, and poetry. The selection in this anthology is an excerpt from *Justice Is Love*, her memoir-in-progress, and part of a linked short story collection based on her extensive research into the ancestors of her extended family. The *Missouri Review* nominated "If It's True, It Must Also Be Beautiful," for inclusion in the Best of the Net anthology; "Cough Drop Joe" won the Colorado Genealogy Society Black Sheep Award; and "Mississippi Goddam" was published in *Valley Voices*, a journal of Mississippi Valley State University. She has two novels set in South Asia, *The Shawl of Midnight* (Golden Antelope Press, 2022) and *My Sisters Made of Light* (Press 53, 2010), which was a finalist for the Colorado Book Award in Literary Fiction. She has a law degree and Masters in Creative Writing, served as a Denver County Judge, and she was counsel to the Rename St*pleton for All project.

A recent graduate from Colorado State University in Fort Collins, CO, **Charlotte Suttee** is currently exploring South America. Her speculative fiction novel, *Weather and Beasts and Growing Things*, is available online and in bookstores September 2023. Her hobbies include eating fresh fruit, watching independent cinema, and talking to the local animals. Other poems by Charlotte are found in various Colorado anthologies.

Valerie A. Szarek is an award-winning performance poet and Native American flute player. She was named "Poet of the Year" Blissfest and has won the Colorado Author's League best poem award three times. Valerie offers "Writing as Ceremony" workshops monthly. She owns Breezy Mountain Leather as well as a Shamanic healing practice. She has four books of poetry. www.poetval.com.

Tara Szkutnik is a Gemini rising whose compulsion to overshare is rewarded in the right venue, yet punished when her daughters swear in public. Her photography and poetry have recently appeared in the art and literary journal, *The Progenitor*. Read more of her writing at LostSoulAstrology.com and medium.com/@lostsoulastrology.

Celia Turner is a Loveland poet who has participated in the Grind for years. She continues to enlarge her poetry brain with workshops and readings and is delighted to have found this special means of communication.

Linda Whittenberg went from writing sermons to writing poems after retiring from the Unitarian Universalist ministry. Most any day she is up before the birds stir to see what words appear. The result has been five collections—the first, *Tender Harvest*, a finalist for the New Mexico book award. Her work also appears in many journals and anthologies.

Acknowledgments

As always, this anthology could not have been brought to fruition without the hard work and commitment of so many people.

First and foremost, thanks to all of the writers and poets who contributed their thoughts and works to our exploration of what it means to be normal. When we proposed this theme, we knew the responses would be beyond what we could imagine, and our contributors did not disappoint. Each piece blossomed into a different interpretation of normalcy, and the fruit of their labors is rich.

More thanks to Leia Sage Creations for designing our cover. Many of the selected pieces incorporated trees in some way, and we felt we needed an arboreal cover. Leia beautifully captured many of the anthology's themes with her rich, vivid imagery.

Whittling down a forest of submissions is never easy, and our editorial team only survived thanks to the first-round work of Miranda Birt, Ronda Simmons, JC Lynne, and Amy Rivers. And we very much appreciate the initial communications and organizational work of our erstwhile submissions coordinator, Krystapher Ardrey. We miss them and wish they hadn't moved so far away!

Lead editors Lorrie Wolfe and Bonnie McKnight once again led the editorial team through hours and months of painstaking work selecting, pruning, and cultivating the thirty-seven poems and over twenty-eight thousand words of prose of the final anthology. Thank you to Sarah Roberts for being there with us every step of the way.

And many thanks to Jack Martin and Kathleen Willard for bringing their poetic know-how to the critical task of poetry selection. And to all who lent a proofreading eye to the final product, especially Suzanne Duvall of Purple Pencil Proofreading, LLC, and Mallory Wilson, thank you!

Amy Rivers deserves special acknowledgment for continuing to prioritize paid publishing opportunities for writers by orchestrating the massive undertaking that is this anthology. This anthology exists because of her vision and leadership. And with her nurturing guidance, each anthology exceeds expectations.

And last but not least, thank you to What If? Publishing for taking over the task of internal layout and formatting of the final product. You took a load off Amy's back and delivered a lovely final harvest.

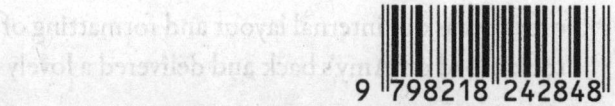